MW01630064
ICE land

Santa Claus
COLLECTION

COLLECTION

Volume 7
Meredith® Books
Des Moines, Iowa

The FACES of Santa

Santa comes with many faces and in many styles but always touches our heart. Whether we see him fashioned of clay and cloth, carved from wood and painted to a fine finish, made of well-worn tin, or any other imaginable way, we know that these replicas of Santa Claus fill our hearts with joy and make us smile.

In this book all about Santa, you'll be amazed at the history and customs about him all around the world. The collections you see are truly inspiring—almost as inspiring as the people who cherish their special pieces. The craftspeople and artists have talent beyond imagination. So sit back and get ready for some fun as you look at the many faces of Santa.

Opposite: *Crafted from clay, carved from wood, or collected and preserved for decades, Santa comes in all styles and shapes.* Above: *A well-worn vintage tin toy portrays Santa in his sleigh.*

Table of Contents

8 LASTING LEGENDS

10 Santa School

14 With a Deft Touch of Hand

22 All Dressed in Red

26 TIMELESS MEMORABILIA

28 The Glow of Santa

32 The Most Famous Reindeer of All

36 DEVOTED COLLECTORS

38 Sweet Santa

48 With Love, From Santa

54 Evelyn's House of Santas

62 MASTER CRAFTERS

64 A Touch of Holly

72 Old World Appeal

82 What a Ride with Santa

92 A Very Mary Christmas

102 From the Heart Art

110 The Eyes Have It

122 The Folk Art Factor

132 Pieces of the Past

140 A Story for the Children

144 PERSONAL EXPRESSIONS & SWEET SENSATIONS

158 SOURCES

Opposite: *Jim Shore's amazingly embellished Santas stand together and smile.*

Brian Pilkington shares the Icelandic Santa legend by creating the 13 Yule Lad Santas each with their own unique story.

The story of Santa Claus has filled our hearts and souls for generations. All across the globe, Santa's story touches us as no other while we anticipate the holidays and the Jolly Old Elf himself.

Lasting Legends

HOME OF THE
Famous Santa Claus School
CHARLES W. HOWARD, Dean
The ONLY SCHOOL of its kind in the WORLD
Home of the Famous Santa Claus School
Albion, New York

HOME OF THE
Famous Santa Claus School
CHARLES W. HOWARD, Dean
ONLY SCHOOL of its kind IN THE WORLD

Santa School

WHILE THERE'S ONLY ONE "REAL" SANTA, HUNDREDS OF OTHERS ARE LEARNING TO EMULATE HIS JOVIAL CHARACTER AND IMPRESSIONABLE STYLE.

Being Santa is not a job; it's a privilege. Since 1937, this has been the motto of the Charles W. Howard Santa Claus School now in Midland, Michigan (120 miles north of Detroit). Here, about 70 students gather yearly, for three intense days in mid-October, to learn the ways of the Merry Man and deliver his spirit to the rest of the world.

These people do not enroll for money or fame, but simply to represent Santa authentically. According to headmaster Tom Valent, "Our student Clauses work

Opposite, above: *Beginning in 1937, a handful of students convened yearly in the Howard family home in Albion, New York (35 miles west of Rochester). The school has since moved to Midland, Michigan.* Opposite, below: *Santa Claus School meets in the Santa House, a 1,200-square-foot, two-building wonderland donated and maintained by the Midland Foundation, a nonprofit community organization.* Right: *As the first Macy's Santa, founder of the world's first Santa School, toy maker, and designer of the "real" Santa suit, Charles W. Howard embodied the passion, love, and spirit of Santa himself.*

Written by Judith Stern Friedman ✦ Postcards and photos, courtesy Ken McPherson and Thomas F. Valent

from the heart, from all different walks of life." Many appear publicly, and others come simply to be more believable among family and friends. Since the real Santa can't be everywhere at once, these aspiring students are Santas-in-training—learning every aspect of his being and hoping to absorb a piece of the magic.

FUNDAMENTAL LESSONS

From the minute Santa Claus School begins, students understand this is serious business. Following a morning meet-and-greet session, class begins with a survey of Santa Claus history and legends, from covering Santa's European roots to memorizing every reindeer's name. They also address children's high expectations. "Santa has to be great and attentive," Valent says, "with the right dress, the right makeup, and fresh breath. Whether children are the first or last ones on your lap, you have to make them feel like the most special children in the world."

Twelve guest experts come to the school to help build important Santa skills, including practicing "ho-ho-ho," storytelling, signing, and interviewing the visually impaired. Real-live reindeer Cupid and Comet also offer hands-on demonstrations. "We develop a North Pole image," Valent explains. Students can see and feed the animals, as well as learn about their gregarious nature.

Then there is hands-on flight experience. In an adjoining warehouse that simulates a starry sky, nine animated reindeer pull a 44-foot long sleigh, and every Santa student rides. The group also visits a Frankenmuth, Michigan, toy store and shares in a night of Christmas song. A graduation banquet marks the course's end, which students agree always comes too soon. Many return year after year to share their experiences as honorable Santa's helpers.

LASTING LEGACY

Tom Valent and his wife, Holly, credit Charles W. Howard, who began this vision of a virtuous, credible Santa. A farmer and later a toy maker by trade, Howard's 16 years as Macy's first Santa inspired him to start the school in 1937 from his Albion, New York, farm. In addition to writing a Santa standards manual, he designed the first "real" Santa suit (see "All Dressed in Red," page 23) and turned his farm into a public Christmas Park, complete with real reindeer, a holiday train, and of course, main-attraction Santa visits.

When Howard passed away in 1966, he entrusted the school to Nate and Mary Ida Doan, who for a decade had been avid Santa students. After five years continuing at the farmhouse, the Doans moved the school to Bay City, Michigan. Mary Ida Doan says, "We gave the students lots of personal attention. The camaraderie was fantastic."

Then in 1987, Tom and Holly Valent accepted the torch (Tom had been a Santa since 1976) and embraced the school with the same loving arms. Today, they groom Santas all over the US and internationally. Other Santa schools are established as well, including one in London and another in Canada, led by enthusiast Victor Nevada. "We give people the ability to change people's lives in a positive way," he says.

When students graduate, emotions run high for all of the warmth and closeness they feel. "In the end, we eat a lot of milk and cookies," Valent laughs. Among the countless lessons they learn, they realize Santa doesn't slide down the chimney; he enters through people's hearts.

Opposite: *Charles Howard and Mrs. Santa at the Santa school.* Right: *Graduates of the Santa school gather before they begin their exciting roles playing Santa around the world.*

WITH A DEFT TOUCH OF HAND

WHAT BETTER PLACE TO HAVE MORE THAN ONE SANTA THAN IN ICELAND—A MAGICAL LAND INDEED.

Written by Carol McGarvey ✦ Illustrations by Brian Pilkington
Photographs by Andy Lyons

Giljagaur stays in barns and steals milk. He is the second yule lad to arrive.

Stúfur or Stubby is only about 2 feet tall and is the third yule lad to arrive with gifts for the children. A small toy, candy, or fruit is left in the child's shoe—unless the child has been bad—then he leaves a potato!

Understanding the legend, the lore, and the magic of Christmas can be a bit overwhelming, especially in Iceland, where Santa Claus takes on many interpretations. One who is up to the task is illustrator Brian Pilkington, a transplant from Liverpool, England. "I came here on holiday after college, and I have never left," he explains. "Deep down, I'd have to say that I'm still on holiday many years later."

Brian became fascinated by the legends and the lore of Iceland, a country where tradition stays intact because of its isolated location. "This country is fantastic and strange, and because of its isolation for centuries, it has maintained many of it's traditional customs." Until technology connected Icelanders with the rest of the world in recent years by the Internet, Sky TV, and an increasing number of tourists, the people weren't exposed to too many foreign ideas, he points out.

Þvorusleikir is called the spoon licker. He brings gifts to the children but his first love is to lick the spoons after delicious Christmas baking.

Ketkrokur loves to steal meat and carries a meathook with him all the time!

"We had TV two hours a day and never on Thursday," he says, "so there was pretty limited exposure to the rest of the world."

The freelance artist has published 20 books, mostly for children. One that is particularly geared to the Christmas season is *The Yule Lads: A Celebration of Iceland's Christmas Folklore.* Brian, who lives in Reykjavik, spent months and months on the research and writing, in addition to the artwork.

The book tells the enchanting stories of the Yule Lads, 13 little rascals who add whimsy and fun to the season. Brian mentions an interesting point. "The pagan word for this period of the year was Jól, the Icelandic word for Christmas. That's "yule" in English. It might also be related to the English word jolly."

Gluggagægir is a shifty character always on the lookout for little knick knacks he can steal. He makes funny faces to make himself look scary.

Evil-looking Gryla and Leppaludi are the troll parents of the lads—bad children beware!

The Yule Lads for centuries have been little imps and devils, and Brian interpreted them in an intense graphic manner for the book. "This book is as authentic as possible. I get inside their heads with all my research. It's an interesting alternative to the usual Santa Christmas story." With bulbous noses and piercing eyes, the lads have specialties—slamming doors, licking bowls, stealing sausage, and the like.

Perhaps it's the cold weather or the country's somewhat mysterious landscape, but Icelanders have a fine literary imagination, Brian believes. Icelandic folk stories are full of ogres, monsters, and trolls, just the perfect subject matter for the illustrator.

Skyrgamur loves to eat the Icelandic answer to yogurt—Skur. He is quite a glutton.

Gryla and Leppaludi, the troll parents of the lads, became "threat material" to Icelandic parents, as in a warning to misbehaving children. With hairy arms, stringy hair, pointed horns, and hooves for feet, Gryla is a real charmer. Her spouses—there were three—are real cuties with big noses, hairy eyebrows, missing teeth, and sinister looks.

From his research Brian dicovered that grumpy Gryla didn't change much over the centuries, but her sons have had a transformation over time, going from evil ogres in the 17th century to rascally pilferers by the 19th century. Why, they stopped eating children and started giving out small gifts – one a day for the 13 days before Christmas. "It's a wonderful buildup to the holiday," Brian says.

Bjugnakraekir is known as the sausage stealer—always looking for goodies for himself.

Brian Pilkington has been illustrating books and creating magic figures for more than 20 years. His amazing illustrations and figurines bring smiles to all who see them.

Skekkjarstaur loves sheep—so common in Iceland. Like his brothers, he leaves small gifts in each child's shoe.

And what's the deal with footwear and Christmas, Brian wonders. Icelandic children leave their shoes on the windowsill, while other youngsters around the world leave out wooden shoes or stockings hung with care. In Iceland, children receive a small toy, a piece of fruit, or a sweet treat. Less-than-nice children receive a potato.

Brian has published other holiday books for children, and he enjoys dreaming up whimsical characters to draw. Topics of other books include a troll trilogy and a folklore book of the "hidden people" who live in rocks and caves and have magical powers. "You can't believe how mystical the folklore is here." It's perfect for the talented illustrator with a big imagination himself.

He mostly works in watercolor on colored paper. "I don't like to work on white paper at all," he insists.

"You know, Christmas will always be special, because it is aimed at children. There's always a new audience, so it will always be wonderful and always be special."

Brian and his wife Kate, who also came from England, are busy with two young sons. Brian also has a daughter, who made him a grandfather not long ago. Kate plays viola in the Icelandic Symphony.

Aside from studying and researching the rich folklore of his adopted country, Brian tries to learn the complex Icelandic language. "It's hard for non-natives who didn't study it or grow up practicing it," he says. "Plus, it's hard to learn, because of the intricacies. For example, a word like house might have 16 different words—for in the house, in front of the house, behind the house, around the house, and many

Pottasleikir loves to eat any leftovers at Christmastime.

Askasleikir loves to eat out of his own bowl—it is wooden with a hinged lid.

more. Really, the only word that's in English is on the roads—STOP."

In addition to the lads, Icelandic children must also contend with the Yule Cat, who watches to make sure that children get a new item of clothing each Christmas. Brian interpreted the feline with sinister eyes and sharp fangs and claws, not exactly a fuzzy little kitten.

Besides his work on paper, Brian has developed a line of five-inch resin figurines of the 13 Yule Lads to accompany the book and to further share the legend of the characters.

Gáttapefur or Doorsniffer, loves smelling sweet Christmas breads.

Kertasnikir or Candle beggar steals candles—a traditional gift given on December 24 each year.

Hurdaskellir or Door Slammer is really a frustrated percussionist and loves to make noise—even when he is bringing gifts.

Yule Time in Iceland

CAN YOU IMAGINE DEALING WITH 13 SANTAS?

In the North Atlantic country of Iceland, where stars often twinkle during daytime because of long winter nights, the concept of Santa Claus takes a different twist.

Keeping up with one Santa Claus figure is tough enough—and fun enough—for most people. But can you imagine dealing with 13 of them? That's the task of Icelanders, who refer to them as the Yule Lads or the Yule Men.

According to a 13th-century legend, there were two ogres who lived in the mountains. The woman was known as Gryla, and her husband was called Leppaludi. Because her husband was bedridden, Gryla was known to go from house to house, begging food along the way. At Christmastime, legend says that she stole children who had misbehaved. However in 1746 the king of Iceland forbade the telling of this folktale. From that time on, the children, called Jolasveinar or Christmas Boys, of the two ogres became associated with the holiday season.

In many cultures, these little creatures, part troll and part prankster, have taken on a secondary role, as elves or Santa's helpers. But in Iceland, they have a stronger status. Dressed in red or in native Icelandic costumes, they come down from the mountains one at a time, starting December 13.

Originally, they were known to play tricks on the townspeople or to beg food or candles. Plus, they were a little bit scary. Today, however, they are known to give gifts. For 13 days, they leave gifts in children's shoes, which are placed on the windowsill if the child has behaved well. For bad behavior, the Yule Men leave a potato or other not-so-fun items. The Jolasveinar start returning to the mountains on Christmas Day, one at a time, until the last one leaves on January 6.

Some folklorists use ancient names with many syllables for the impish crew, but contemporary names focus on their specialties. Would you believe Sheepfold Stick, Gully Oak, Pan-Scraper, Spoon-Licker, Pot-Licker, Bowl-Licker, Door-Slammer, Curd Glutton, Sausage Pilferer, Peeper, Sniffer, Meat Hook, and Candle Beggar?

The first one, for example, loves sheep's milk. Gully Oak has a fetish for the froth on milk, so he hangs out with the cows. The next ones, respectively, keep close watch on pans, spoons, pots, and bowls. You'd be amazed at how much food is left in those vessels!

Door-Slammer loves to do his thing when people are sleeping, while Curd Glutton craves dairy products. Sausage Pilferer or Snatcher loves to climb up into the rafters to steal sausages in the smokehouse. Peeper's first name could possibly be Tom, and he loves to watch people and look in windows for things to steal. Sniffer seeks out fried bread. Meat Hook has been known to put a long pole with a hook on the end down chimneys to retrieve meat hung on poles to cook. Candle Beggar is self-explanatory.

Needless to say, the bunch has the home and barn pretty well covered during the holiday season.

Because of Iceland's geographical position, days are

very short in the winter. It's no wonder then that Icelanders love to decorate with lights at Christmastime. They outline windows, balconies, and rooftops with festive lights, starting on the first Sunday in December. Advent lights, electric candlesticks with seven lights, glow in windows, and wreaths have four candles, one for each Sunday in Advent. The heavily decorated Christmas trees, however, are decorated on St. Thorlakur's Day, December 23, named for Thorlakur Thorhallsson, former Bishop of Skalholt. On that day, families partake of a simple meal of skate, a type of fish.

Traditionally, the tree lights are lit for the first time when Christmas is "chimed in" by every church bell at 6 p.m. on Christmas Eve.

A poignant tradition takes place on the morning of Christmas Eve, a time to remember deceased loved ones. Graves are decorated with boughs of fir or pine and, in many cases, large candles to burn through the night.

As in other cultures, homes buzz with holiday activity in December. Baked items take on special importance. Many families make spiced, gingersnap-like cookies, along with many other varieties.

Another tradition is laufabraud or leaf bread, flat cakes of flour and water fried in oil or mutton fat. The cakes are decorated with a special pattern or "leaves." In times gone by, flour was an imported luxury and used sparingly. So leaf bread dough was rolled out very thin to get as many cakes as possible. Each one was decorated to make it special.

And just like spring cleaning, Icelanders spruce up their homes from top to bottom to prepare for the holidays. They also enjoy making special dinners for family members and friends. Most Icelanders eat pork, ham, or rock ptarmigan on Christmas Eve. Pork and ham are relatively new flavors, which were imported from Denmark. For those who don't have a lamb to slaughter—smoked lamb is the traditional holiday meat—rock ptarmigan, a wild bird, may substitute.

Dessert is often rice pudding. For the holidays, though, it's called almond pudding. An almond is put into the pudding before serving. Whoever gets the almond in his or her portion wins a prize.

Yule gifts were rare until the 19th century. Before that, summer presents were more common. One gift always includes a new piece of clothing for every family member. Tradition has it that those who did not receive a new garment would be captured by the Jolakottur or giant Yule Cat. Not surprisingly, Yule Cat belonged to Gryla, the nasty mother of the Yule Lads. That notion is based on the fact that every effort was made to finish all work with the autumn wool before the Yule season. The reward for those who helped was a new piece of clothing. Those who were lazy received nothing. The threatening story of the Yule Cat was an incentive to get people to work harder. It worked!

Sending Christmas card greetings is also special in Iceland. Sometimes this is the only correspondence with far-flung relatives and friends, so the card is chock-full of good wishes and happy news.

Opposite and Below: *Brian also has a line of 3-dimensional figurines that he has created showing the Yule Lads and their story. These delightful fellows are available on-line at www.sunfilm.is or in Icelandic Christmas shops.*

Santa Claus School
ALBION, N.Y.
Quality Santa Supplies

All Dressed in Red

THE STORY OF SANTA'S SUIT

ONE VISIONARY MAN DESIGNED THE "REAL SUIT" THAT HELPED RAISE RED AND WHITE TO LEGENDARY STATUS.

The modern American image of Santa is synonymous with red and white. Shaped by 19th-century poet Clement Clarke Moore ("'Twas the night before Christmas...") and *Harper's Weekly* caricatures drawn by Thomas Nast, the modern Santa suit has, with its bold, emotional color, become a timeless holiday fashion.

Some attribute Santa's red-and-white style to the Coca-Cola illustrator Haddon Sundblom. His memorable 1930s advertisements decked out Santa in red and white to promote the soft-drink company's colors. Certainly Sundblom's images helped perpetuate the red and white fashion—but others were promoting it just as passionately.

Opposite: *A shiny rayon satin lining—with a convenient hidden pocket—was a signature mark of the Charles W. Howard Santa suit. Every handmade coat also touted a label to declare its authenticity.*

A SENSE OF SANTA STYLE

In the 1930s in Albion, New York (about 35 miles west of Rochester), Macy's first Santa Claus, Charles W. Howard, realized a growing need for quality Santa apparel. With increasing appearances in department stores, parades, movies, ads, and public functions, Santa needed to expand his wardrobe. Mr. Howard extolled the "real" reasons for Santa's red-and-white style: Red represents a healthy outdoorsman, he said, which is also why Santa's cheeks are red. The white fur stands for purity in person, character, and heart.

Howard's motives were not commercial, but rather a true extension of character. He hoped to further Santa's pristine image by designing the best quality Santa apparel available. These early relics were like candy for the eyes: A cherry-red wool-and-nylon coat and pants were lined in luscious, creamy rayon satin. Six-inch-wide, French-white rabbit fur generously trimmed the collar and sleeves; and a red wool hat was trimmed in fur for extra warmth. Wool, Howard said,

Written by Judith Stern Friedman ✦ Photos, courtesy Ken McPherson ✦ Photo, page 25, Bill Covell

is the fabric of Santa because he is an everyday working man—not a king perched on a throne.

Then there was the 5-inch-wide, hand-tooled chrome belt buckle that Mr. Howard designed specifically for the jolly man. Each of four corners came to two separate points—a total of eight—representing Santa's reindeer. Black leather boot tops from a Rochester, New York shoemaker, pure white gloves, and yak hair and beard made in New York City completed the ensemble, all of which were assembled in the Howards' home.

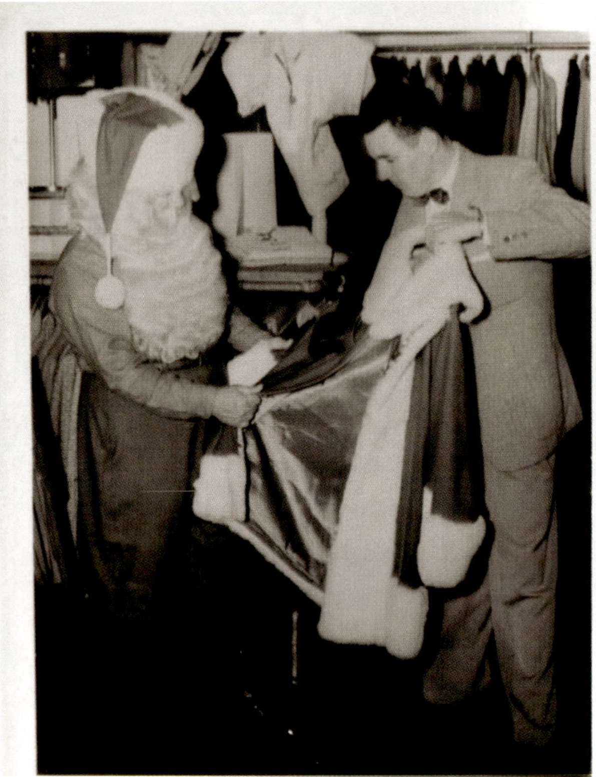

Above: *In this reminder postcard to customers, Charles W. Howard described his vision for Santa fashion: "Supreme comfort, convincing appearance, unusual long wear. You can buy cheaper, but you cannot buy better."* Opposite: *Original Charles W. Howard Santa suits have become true relics of Santa's purity: in person, character, and heart.*

STITCH-FOR-STITCH

Howard's daughter, Gale Bergeman, remembers a woman, Adeline Hill, who lived on her family's farm and helped her father stitch the suits: "She started making them in the corner of our dining room," she recalls. Gale's mother, Ruth, helped repair the suits. Soon they found other "elves" to help them sew—all out of their homes. One seamstress, Elizabeth W. Babcock, cut most of the fabric and eventually bought the business in 1965. "If I made 50 suits a year back then," Elizabeth says, "I was doing well, but it grew way beyond that." In the 1930s, a Santa suit—complete with boots and hair goods—sold for $75. By the 1960s, the ensemble appreciated to $400.

In those days Babcock kept busy year-round repairing, cleaning, and storing Santa suits, then picking up the pace beginning in August, filling hundreds of new orders. Meanwhile Mr. Howard personally took to the road, selling his wares at a few trade shows, by word of mouth, and through direct mail. He also used postcards to remind his customers: "It's time to order your Santa Claus Equipment."

MODERN MATERIAL

With Charles W. Howard's death in 1966 and the escalating costs of raw materials, the suit-making business soon became cost-prohibitive and Elizabeth Babcock resigned her work to history. But Santa's fashions still live on in countless reproductions made more efficiently overseas.

One Belle Vernon, Pennsylvania manufacturer, Halco, has been sewing quality Santa suits in America since the late 1940s. Currently it distributes 45,000 costumes annually—for subsequent sale or rental—to costume companies, talent agencies, chain stores,

PHOTO: BILL COVELL

amusement parks, and Santa helpers worldwide. Suits are available in 15 different styles as short coats, long jackets, suits, or capes, up to a triple-extra large (which fits a 72-inch waist). Fabrics range from lightweight tricot to majestic plush, in cherry red to regal burgundy, retailing from $40 to $800.

Since Charles W. Howard's early vision of a well-dressed Claus, Santa fashion has changed—and yet it hasn't. Countless companies share the market on red and white, but many interpretations don't live up to Howard's standards. Still, the look remains a lasting legend.

Twice as Nice
HANGERS
PAPER NOVELTY MFG. CO., STAMFORD, CONN.

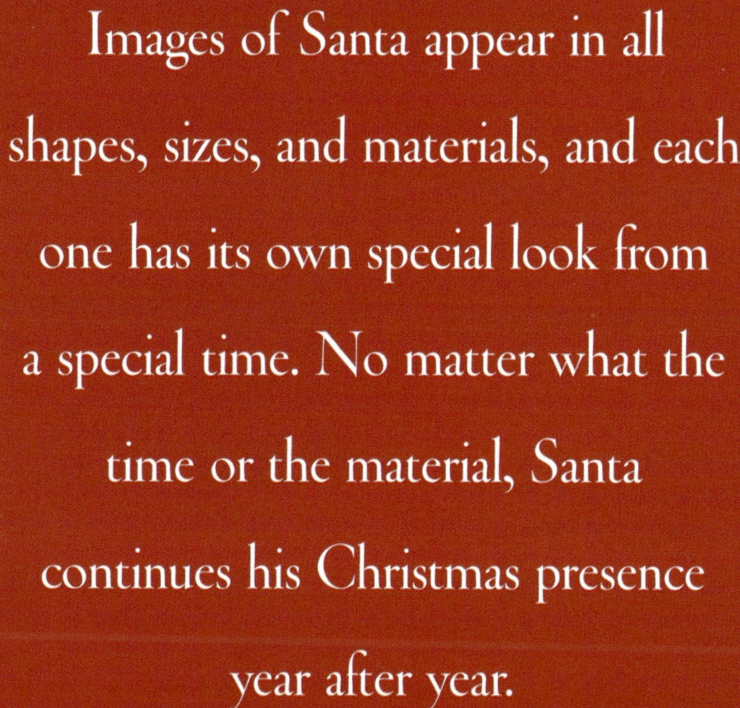

Images of Santa appear in all shapes, sizes, and materials, and each one has its own special look from a special time. No matter what the time or the material, Santa continues his Christmas presence year after year.

TIMELESS MEMORABILIA

Santa candles from the collection of Linda McVicker and Donna Chesnut line up on vintage holiday boxes.

THE GLOW OF SANTA

FOR YEARS SANTA HAS BROUGHT HIS WARM SPIRIT TO EVERY PART OF CHRISTMAS DECORATING.

There's an unmistakable glow when Santa Claus is around. That's especially true when Santa candles are used in holiday decorations. Sometimes they can be tucked into a mantel display or into mixed company with Santa figures made in a variety of media, from papier-mâché to wood and fabric. There are choir boys, singing angels, Christmas tree shapes, and Santa boot candles too.

Opposite: *These vintage Santa candles were never lit so they can be enjoyed for years to come.*

Written by Carol McGarvey ✦ *Photographs by Andy Lyons*

Often Santa-shaped candles are roly-poly, just like the "right Jolly Old Elf" himself. Other Santa candles stand tall and pencil-thin, because they are tapers placed in holders to trim a buffet table of appetizers or a dinner table for a sit-down meal.

Check on eBay, the on-line auction service, and you'll see a fair number of Santa Claus candles. Or peruse tag sales and flea markets. Invariably, you'll find a Santa candle or two in the Christmas decorations mix.

So why are candles still whole, just as they were when they were purchased? That's easy. Think about it.

Conscience prevails. Who wants to light a match to Santa Claus?

Opposite: *Two large Santa candles from the 1950s are still in excellent condition with paint on the wax still in place.* Above: *These happy Santas were made in the 1960s.*

THE MOST FAMOUS Reindeer OF ALL

SANTA IS GRATEFUL FOR HIS FOUR-LEGGED FRIENDS THAT ALWAYS GET HIM WHERE HE NEEDS TO GO.

Opposite: *Reindeer made of plastic and painted silver line up to serve Santa.* Above: *Celluloid and early plastic reindeer from the 1950s portray Rudolph in entirely different poses.*

Nearly everyone can sing the "Rudolph, the Red-Nosed Reindeer" song. Parents pass it along to their children and make sure they watch the television special each year. The phenomenon of Rudolph started out as a marketing technique for the chain of Montgomery Ward department stores, headquartered in Chicago.

Ward stores had been purchasing coloring books to give away to children each holiday season, and the company thought a little personalization would go a long way into charming customers. In 1939, employee Robert L. May, who enjoyed writing children's stories, was chosen to create a holiday booklet.

Tapping into the story of the Ugly Duckling, along with his own memories of being bullied as a child, May focused on a reindeer, out of the loop for reindeer games because of his glowing red nose. Illustrator Denver Gillen of the company's art department went

Written by Carol McGarvey ✦ *Photographs by Andy Lyons*

with May to Lincoln Park Zoo to sketch some deer for the booklet. Although executives were worried that the red nose might be associated with drinking, they approved the story and the drawings. The rest, as they say, is history.

Montgomery Ward stores distributed 2.4 million copies of Rudolph's story in 1939. Even with shortages during World War II, the next several years, nearly 6 million books were distributed by the end of Christmas, 1946.

Wards kept the copyright, and May got no royalties for the story of Rudolph, even though he desperately needed the money for his wife's terminal illness and death. Finally in 1947, company president Sewell Avery turned the copyright over to May.

May's brother-in-law, songwriter Johnny Marks, developed lyrics and a melody. Even though many others turned it down, singing cowboy Gene Autry took a chance, and he sold two million copies that year. It went on to become the best-selling song of its era, second only to "White Christmas." A television special narrated by Burl Ives has become a classic.

In those early days Rudolph guided Santa's sleigh through thick fog. Today, however, there's another reason to have Rudolph in the lead—his shiny nose helps weather experts track Santa's progress on Christmas Eve.

Opposite: *Reindeer in rich browns stand in front of this 1930 calendar with embossed reindeer on the front.* Above: *Rudolph comes in all kinds of items including this mold and toy from the 1950s.* Right: *Holiday music often featured Rudolph as a star.*

YOU GO, GIRLS!

P.S. In some circles, there seems to be some controversy about Santa's other reindeer, according to some sources. You know, Dasher and Dancer and Prancer and Vixen and Comet and Cupid and Donner and Blitzen. Well some purists speculate that there's a possibility that they might all be female! Many males of the species shed their antlers in November and early December, while females don't lose their antlers until after they give birth in the spring. Since all the drawings of the reindeer show full antlers, there's some question.

In any event, over the years, reindeer have been depicted in metal, papier-mâché, wood, straw, and plastic, from large enough to stand on the front porch to tiny enough to be part of a tabletop display.

1950s advertising Santas from Evelyn Schirms's collection pose together.

Preserving the memory of the Jolly Old Elf by collecting his magical image, these Santa Claus collectors keep his presence near them to share with Santa lovers everywhere.

Devoted Collectors

SWEET SANTA

WHETHER IT BE CHOCOLATE MOLDS OR CANDY CONTAINERS, WENDY MULLEN FINDS THE SWEET SIDE OF SANTA.

Some collectors display their antiques collections in shadow boxes, on shelves, or in groupings for decorative impact. That's all well and good. But for Wendy Mullen of San Juan Bautista, California, it's important not only to love her numerous antique chocolate molds and German candy containers, but to use them as well.

Depending on the season or the holiday at hand, the busy mother of five pulls out a batch of her molds and makes chocolate, just to have fun with the kids. She also has learned to use the same molds to fashion chalkware pieces.

"About 16 years ago, I became aware of old chocolate molds in a shop in San Jose, where I was taking a cake

Opposite: *Rare Santa candy containers found their way to Wendy Mullen's home.* Above: *This unusual chocolate Santa mold comes in three sections.* Above, right: *The bottom of the candy container pulls out revealing candy inside.*

Written by Carol McGarvey ✦ *Photographs by Jay Wilde*

SOLID
NICKEL
SILVER
55

16596
18

decorating class. I saw a mold on display in the store, and I immediately fell in love with it," she explains. "The owner said, 'If you ever see one, buy it.' Now remember, this is in the time period before the Internet or eBay. Not long after, I was in an antiques barn, and I saw some hinged bunny molds for $45. Of course, I made a purchase."

Not long after that eBay started, and Wendy began her quest for molds in earnest. "They were pretty scarce, but I did buy 10 molds from a woman on the East Coast. Remember, at its beginning, eBay was not international, so I was limited to the United States."

Later, when it did go worldwide, Wendy was one of three people bidding on a 1,500-piece collection in Belgium. The other two bidders lived in Europe, so she got pieces that the other two didn't want. "I didn't have a passport, so I couldn't go in person. However, I did request an 11-inch teddy bear mold, some Victorian children molds, and a 20-inch St. Nick. I was hooked for real," she says.

Opposite: *Antique tin Santa molds in all sizes and shapes are a part of Wendy's collection.* Above: *Wendy shows one of her candy containers.* Above, right: *A rare collection of Santa molds is displayed together.*

Her quest continued, and she now has about 500 chocolate molds. By way of explanation, Wendy says chocolate molds are often made of tin and are sometimes hinged. She likes them because the detailed design is visible on the outside, just as the chocolate piece will appear. Ice cream molds, on the other hand, usually are pewter, and the design is on the inside of the piece to form the design on the ice cream. So much of the finished design is not visible on the outside of the mold.

Wendy found that not much had been written about the history of chocolate molds, so she decided to write a book. Printed in 2002, her book is *The Collector's Guide to Antique Chocolate Molds* (Hobby House). It is no longer in print. A second book, *Chocolate Molds: The Comprehensive Guide*, was recently released (Schiffer).

Wendy has learned that the heyday for making chocolate molds was from the late 1800s through the early 1900s by French and German companies such as Maison Pinat, Maison Cadot, and Jean-Baptiste Létang in France, and Hermann Walter and Anton Reiche in Germany.

"Artists sketched detailed designs for chocolate molds and sculpted the figures in a plaster-like material," Wendy explains. "The sculpted piece was cut in half so that a metal casting or 'die' could be made after a molten liquid was poured into the impressions."

The cast pieces were marked with the company's logo, name, and a design number. Wendy says that when looking at molds to buy, collectors should be sure that the design number on one piece of the mold matches the number on the other half. "If you're using it for display only, that's not so important. But if you really want to make chocolate in a mold, the numbers need to match, or the outcome won't be so easy to achieve if the two halves don't match exactly."

Chalkware made in molds

Chocolate molds also were used to make chalkware pieces. When Wendy wanted to learn how to do that process, she contacted artist Penny Byrnes, from Napa Valley, California. In exchange for teaching Penny how to use the Internet, Penny taught Wendy how to paint chalkware Santas and other pieces made from art plaster, available at crafts stores. They use acrylic paints to finish the chalky pieces. "I have learned the importance of good quality brushes," Wendy says.

Wendy has had so much fun painting chalkware pieces and tucking them into areas of the 1883 fixer-upper Victorian home on which she and her husband Patrick are working. For example, she has made chalkware Santas that look just like chocolate candy ones, because of the shiny brown paint she uses. Another Santa, painted in antique gold, stands among Wendy's collection of yellow ware bowls. Soaps and candles also may be made from the old molds.

The Anton Reiche factory alone was known to have thousands of workers and more than 50,000 detailed designs.

After around 1880, the idea spread to the United States. Companies such as Jaburg, the American Chocolate Mould Company, Eppelsheimer, and the Allmetal Chocolate Mold Company got into the design business. Molds were fashioned from copper, nickel, and tin-plated steel.

When plastics took over, fewer metal molds were made, although a few companies still produce them

Above: *Some of Wendy's most unusual Santa molds show Santa on a donkey or with other animals.* Right: *A Santa candy container sits in a pinecone-shaped vehicle.*

today. Therefore, the sky's the limit on prices on the early molds, Wendy points out. Items might range from $75 to $700 and above, depending on their scarcity.

As a result of Wendy's first book, she received a fax one day from the great granddaughter of Anton Reiche. She invited Wendy to Vienna, Austria, to see her great-grandfather's chocolate molds. "What an amazing trip," Wendy exclaims. "I stayed in a castle and was able to see some of the original catalogs and ledgers up close. The factory had been bombed during World War II. I was able to photograph so many of his samples. It was wonderful."

Wendy says she seems to have an eye for appraising the molds and has been called on to do that for other collectors. Her own elusive mold, the one she'd really like to find, shows Santa Claus and an angel baking cookies.

While she still enjoys the hunt for certain molds, she marvels about the molds' original purpose. "They were made just for kids to have fun at Christmas, Easter, Halloween, and any other time of the year. It's really amazing," says the mother of five, from ages 7 to 20.

She also appreciates the whimsy of the designs—Santa sitting on a donkey or Santa riding a running rabbit. Plus a number of the molds have a hole on one side of the design. "That's for holding an accessory, such as Santa holding a tree, which adds a whole three-dimensional feature, which is fascinating." Some secular and religious Christmas themes, such as Santa with an angel, are uncommon.

To keep the purpose of the chocolate molds alive, Wendy took classes to become a chocolatier. "Valrhona chocolate is my favorite." For fun or for festive occasions, she and some of her children make chocolate creations, "just because." With tempered chocolate or chocolate melts, they pour the chocolate into mold halves that have been coated with food-safe mold release or oil. They refrigerate the filled molds for 45 minutes, then allow the mold to return to room temperature before removing the chocolate.

"These molds are not fragile," the collector says. "I believe they are meant to be used. So I do."

Opposite: *Many of Wendy's candy containers are still in the original boxes.* Above, right: *This Santa dressed in red is a candy container from about 1920.*

Above and Right: *Wendy has some rare candy containers and is writing a book about them.* Opposite: *Some of the her oldest Santa candy containers were made in the late 1800s.*

GERMAN CANDY CONTAINERS

Wendy's extensive Santa collection also includes some 300 antique candy containers, most from Germany. In like manner to the molds, someone at a mold company in Germany saw her book and invited her to come for a visit to an old candy container factory. "In three days, I took more than 2,000 photos, and it was fabulous." She learned that the molds for the containers often resembled bricks. Those bricks often were later used for building homes in the area of the factory, making for some interesting details.

Wendy learned that the containers, which come apart to show a small compartment inside for hiding a piece of candy or a small treasure, were first manufactured in Sonneberg, Germany, about 1819.

"They were created for use at all holidays, from Christmas and Easter to Halloween and Thanksgiving," she explains. Early ones were fashioned from flour and paste, which didn't last. Later there was a switch to papier-mâché.

Typically whole families would work on the containers in a cottage-industry operation, and silk, fancy buttons, fur, and fabric were used to embellish the 12-inch-tall containers. Around 1895, the containers started being exported to the United States and were sold in candy shops and major department stores. The ones marketed to Americans often featured political themes. Only two companies in Germany still make the containers.

Wendy owns many rare candy containers. Her oldest ones were made in the late 1880s, and her largest one is extra tall at 20 inches. Most in her collection are from the 1920s.

With Love, From Santa

THE SPIRIT OF GIVING IS ALIVE AND WELL IN THIS HOUSE FILLED WITH SPECIAL SANTAS OF ALL KINDS.

Mike Seifert knows how to touch the heart of his wife Pat at Christmastime. In 1974 he gave her a two-piece Santa Claus votive by Fenton, which sanctioned her collecting bug. Since then, he has commissioned interesting Santas to give as gifts to her. He has arranged for five surprise commissions and always keeps his eye out for the next one.

And instead of resisting her passion for collecting Santa figures, he joins in. Together the Urbandale, Iowa, couple, married for 30 years, scours craft shows, antiques shops, and artists' haunts for unusual varieties.

Pat has amassed nearly 400 statuary-style Santa figures, along with 113 ornaments, which grace the real tree in the living room each holiday season. "Santa represents to me the wonder and surprise of Christmas," Pat explains. "It's all about the spirit of

Above: *Pat's first Santa that started the collecting bug.* Below: *Santas appear on every possible surface and are created from every material. Pat has Santas painted on okra, rocks, and Santas carved from soap.*

Written by Carol McGarvey ✦ *Photographs by Jay Wilde*

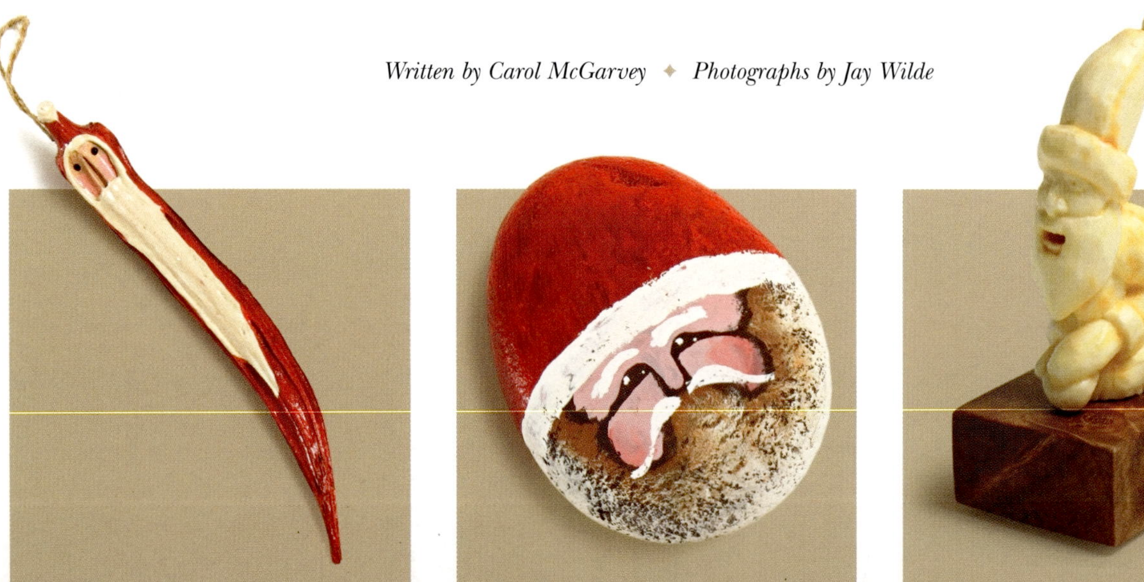

Above: *Pat purchased these antique Santas because they have a special look or appeal.* Below: *A vintage Coke bottle was painted to look like Santa.*

giving. Getting a new Santa for me is like experiencing Christmas morning all over again. It's just special."

For that reason she only keeps a few out all year. Then, when she opens the numerous storage boxes each December, she is surprised all over again.

Early in her collecting, Pat purchased several mass-produced Santa figures. Plus, friends often gave her Santa Claus items as gifts. "But it just got to be too much. Now if I purchase any item that is mass produced, I only get one from that artist as a representative. It is much more important now to search for one-of-a-kind items made from a variety of media."

She now has Santas made of wood, textiles, glass, ceramic, driftwood, cast iron, concrete, papier-mâché, and gourds. There are others made of candle wax, wool, beeswax, lead, brass, silver, glass, pewter, and corncobs. There are more Santas painted on items such as a tea bag, a piece of okra, an oyster shell, a sand dollar, a tongue depressor, a starfish, a vintage Coke bottle, and a shotgun shell. And, yes, there's a Santa painted on a paint brush.

An interesting Santa that Pat commissioned was created by artist Cheryl Smeja of Mineral

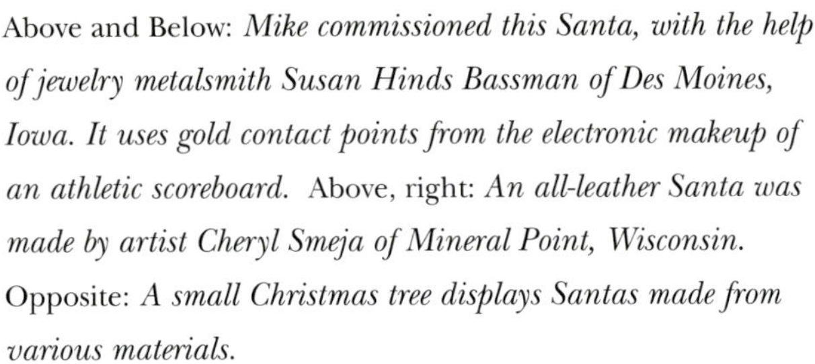

Above and Below: *Mike commissioned this Santa, with the help of jewelry metalsmith Susan Hinds Bassman of Des Moines, Iowa. It uses gold contact points from the electronic makeup of an athletic scoreboard.* Above, right: *An all-leather Santa was made by artist Cheryl Smeja of Mineral Point, Wisconsin.* Opposite: *A small Christmas tree displays Santas made from various materials.*

Point, Wisconsin. Pat met Cheryl on the annual Wisconsin Fall Art Tour, where visitors tour artists' studios around the southwestern part of the state. The Santa figure is made completely of leather, down to his fingernails and eyelids. "Cheryl made dolls, but had never fashioned a Santa before," Pat says. "I'm thrilled with the results." That Santa arrived, appropriately enough, on Christmas Eve.

A special Santa from Mike is, well, worth its weight in gold. A relative who worked for an athletic scoreboard company gave Mike discarded gold contact points used in the electronic makeup of the unit, 40,000 of them, connected in a wire-like coil. Only about 10 percent of each of the tips is gold. Mike carefully snipped off the ends of the tips and took

them to a jewelry metalsmith.

"This got a bit scary along the way," Mike explains. "Before the Santa figure could be cast in Kalona, Iowa, I had to sign that I would pay for any damage if the metal ruined the equipment. Of course, no one knew what other kinds of metal might be in with the gold, so it could have harmed the equipment."

The resulting figure, which also arrived on Christmas Eve, is about nine inches tall and feels as if he should weigh far more than his 10 pounds, because of the density. As it ages, it takes on a green patina, just right for the holiday season.

Pat's oldest Santa is a 1920s era electric Santa light bulb. Another ornament, suspected to be about the same age, is from Germany. It's a Santa with a body made of a mesh bag filled with nuts. The smallest Santa she owns is made of resin and is about the size of a chocolate chip.

The largest Santa in the house greets visitors at the front door. He's a four-foot Santa fashioned from a telephone pole by folk artist Lee Middleswart of Indianola, Iowa (see page 102).

The Seiferts also commissioned Lee to create a favorite Santa. "Some years ago my parents gave us some money, which we used to purchase a Newport flowering plum tree for our yard," Pat explains. "Shortly after my father died, the tree died. A little knot in the tree had the semblance of a face. We asked Lee to create a Santa for us honoring my father by using part of the tree."

Above: *The fishing Santa was created by Iowa artist Lee Middleswart.* Below: *A vintage Santa cookie box, an antique Santa light bulb, and a large Santa face with movable eyes are among the older pieces that Pat has in her collection.*

And so she did. As the youngest child in her family, Pat often went ice fishing with her dad, so the Santa is carrying a fishing pole and has lures on his hat. The body is fashioned from an old mailbox holder, and because her father was in the feed, grain, and poultry business, that occupation is acknowledged on the back of the Santa with small poultry photos on a door hinge.

"Also, because my dad is now an angel in heaven, this Santa has wooden folk art wings. It's very special to me," says a loving daughter.

Mike's gift last year was a chocolate mold in the shape of Santa Claus. "We were at a show and we always separate for a time to look around. I try to see what I think Pat would pick out as an interesting piece. I spotted the mold, and later, she eyed it too. I had a friend distract her while I purchased it. When she came back around that aisle and it was gone, she was so upset she hadn't bought it. Needless to say, she was very surprised to receive it at Christmas."

Mike has commissioned five Santas for his wife, but is careful to dodge questions about what he might have up his sleeve for the next one.

Mike, a pharmacist, and Pat, a freelance graphic artist, acknowledge that a super–special Santa was made out of plastic Legos by their son, Geoff, soon to be a pharmacist himself (a fourth-generation one, in fact). Geoff gave it to Pat one holiday season when he was a little guy.

Above: *Pat poses with her husband Mike in their home full of Santa Claus figures. Mike endears himself to his wife by commissioning special pieces to be made for her.* Left: *Made entirely from clay, this Santa stands about a foot tall.*

What is she looking for next? Pat saw a Santa carved from a wooden fishing buoy that intrigues her. Now that's one of a kind.

And as for Mike commissioning special pieces for his wife, well, that brings a special twinkle to her eyes. "He's one of a kind, too."

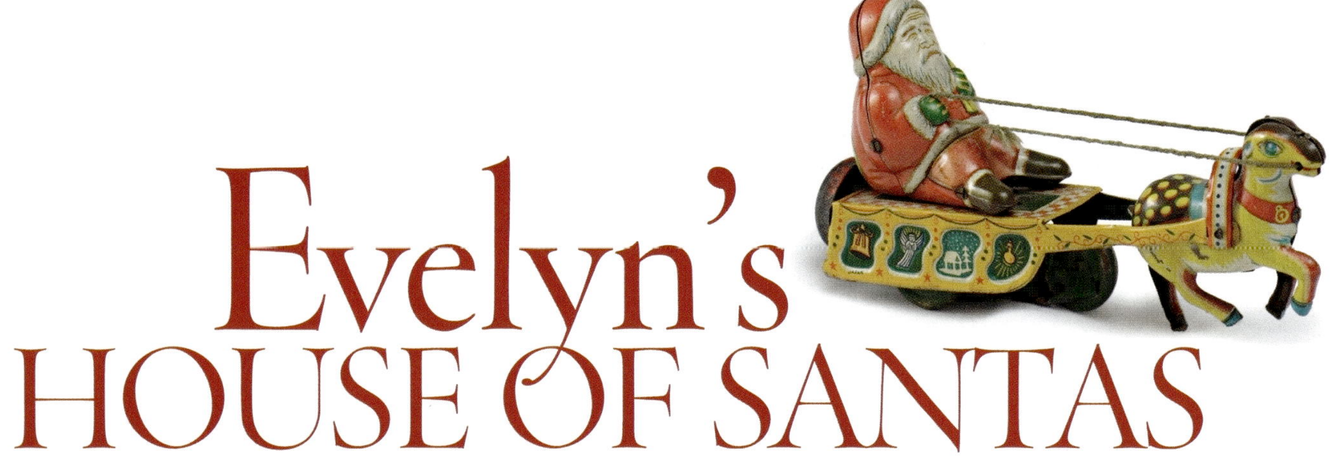

Evelyn's HOUSE OF SANTAS

Above: *A vintage Santa stands at the door of a white house on Evelyn Schirm's mantel.* Opposite: *A sea of Santas from the 1950s that used to be store displays pose together.*

IN EVERY CORNER OF THE HOUSE YOU'LL FIND A JOLLY SANTA THAT EVELYN JUST COULDN'T LEAVE BEHIND.

There are Santa Claus figures at every turn in Evelyn Schirm's home in Urbandale, Iowa, and that's not even at Christmastime!

With nearly 800 holiday pieces, it's hard not to get the Christmas spirit when you visit Evelyn, a veteran collector who knows what she likes. "The Santa pieces are special, and they call out to me. All they have to say is 'take me home,' and I fall for it," she says. Without a doubt, she has answered the call many times.

Her love of all things Christmas was sparked by two events in the 1970s. Her brother gave her a Gorham spoon made into a ring. It had a "Night Before Christmas" scene on it. At about the same time, she started taking antiques classes from a knowledgeable antiques dealer and appraiser in her area. "We were in her home, filled with wonderful antiques. I was fascinated by her Christmas trees of all sizes in every

Written by Carol McGarvey ✦ *Photographs by Scott Little*

Above: *A cloth Santa, a baby rattle Santa, and a small Santa hatbox are among the fascinating Santas in Evelyn Schirm's collection.* Opposite: *A plastic Santa from the 1960s and a larger dressed Santa from the 1940s are among her favorites. Evelyn poses with her Santas.*

room of her home," says Evelyn. "I loved the trees in the bedrooms. I decided that I could do that, too, and I was hooked." Evelyn now has 11 trees up at Christmas and several year-round.

After those classes, she started scouring antiques shops and auctions for holiday items. "Santa figures must pass the personality test with me. They must have a happy face. Christmas is all about the spirit of giving, and they must show that."

From a spectacular feather tree from around the late 1800s, which stays out all year, to a large collection of classic plastic pieces from the 1950s, Evelyn can follow the history of Christmas in marketing pieces and various mediums. There are porcelain, papier-mâché, fabric, fur, and ceramic items.

"Somehow they just seem to multiply from year to year," says the collector, who also sets up tag sales with her company, Tag It. While she leaves many pieces on display during the rest of the year, Christmas, of course,

means unpacking box after box of more treasures. "Really, the collection just seems to grow," she giggles.

Evelyn vows that it's time to pare down, but that's tough. "I tried to sell one of the Santas once—the strange one with eyes that light up. He's always been sort of spooky to me. But when I went to sell him, I simply couldn't do it."

She dresses the part too, with a large Santa sweater collection. "Really and truly, I could start in November and wear a different one every day through Christmas, I believe."

A five-cent cotton Santa from Germany was an early purchase at a sale, and some others have cost about $100. "Most, though, aren't that expensive. It's just that when you multiply it out, it gets a little scary." Santas range from 1 inch up to about four feet, which is a Santa dressed in green fur, that Evelyn thinks was part of an advertising campaign for Sprite. An interesting tiny piece is a Santa-themed baby rattle.

Above, top: *Candles from the 1950s come in Santa shapes that fit Evelyn's collection.* Above: *A child's paper hat box shows Santa on the top of the box.* Opposite: *Plastic Santas, Santas with water tummies, and tiny Santas from the early 1900s are just the beginning of Evelyn's collection.*

Evelyn's recent rule is that if a new piece comes in the house, another must go out. "But it's hard to stick by that," she says. Visitors must understand that it's not just Santa Claus items that she collects. There's Flemish art and pieces of rose china. ("It's very feminine and makes me feel good.") There are Native American hatchets and dolls, stretch glass, Bristol glass, Roseville pottery, transferware, old kitchen utensils, green Depression glass, and vintage bottle brush Christmas trees, which, of course, go with the Santa items.

"I also collect swastika items, which people find curious," she says. "Before the Nazis made it represent something else, that design really was a good luck charm for Native Americans, important to me because of my father's Cherokee heritage."

All these collections must mean that husband Bob is most understanding. "A smart woman collector gets her husband to collect something too," Evelyn insists.

"He worked for a tobacco company many years ago, so he collects tobacco-related items."

A practical question begs an answer. How does one dust all these collections? "Here's my secret," Evelyn confesses. "Just don't move anything. Then it takes on its own patina. Every year right before Christmas, we clean everything, especially when it comes to polishing brass, silver, and glass items. That makes everything else look good."

Evelyn feels a responsibility to share her knowledge of antiques. She's a long-time member of a Questers antiques study group, Artifacts and Old Lace. She also helps decorate Terrace Hill, the Iowa governor's mansion, for the holidays.

Plus she loves giving talks to schoolchildren. "It's important that we pass down the history of some of these pieces. Children don't know the origins of items they use. I made butter with one school group, and they were completely fascinated, because they didn't

know where it came from, except the supermarket. The same was true with lighting. And you can imagine the funny faces when I explained what a chamber pot was."

She loves it when her 12-year-old granddaughter's friends come to see all the holiday items. "They are absolutely fascinated, which I love," says Evelyn.

"The whole idea of Santa is about the spirit of giving," says the collector. "We all can be Santa at heart. Sure, we all know the true meaning of Christmas, but this is the fun part."

Above: *Santas and their sleighs from the early 1900s.*
Above, right: *Papier mâché Santa from about 1930.*
Right: *Candy container Santas from the 1930s have bobbing heads and sit among bottle brush trees.*

A Brush With the Past

It's easy to see how the so-called "bottle brush trees" got their name. They do indeed look as if they could be used for a dish-washing task.

It's also no wonder why they were popular as decorations from the 1920s to the '50s and beyond. They were small and fun and worked well with other decorations. These days they're so old that they almost look contemporary. Most trees and the least expensive were made in Japan. Some others were produced in the United States and Germany.

Big trees, real or synthetic, have always held a special place in a holiday home. Because of the tree's enduring popularity, it has been interpreted in feathers, in fabric, in wood, in papier-mâché, in glass ornaments to hang or to clip on bigger trees, and in brushes.

The bristle-style trees were made in various sizes, generally from 1 to 14 inches. Most people used them as accessories for little holiday vignettes around the house.

While the trees generally are green, there are some others. In the 1950s, there were brightly colored ones, in red, blue, pink, and yellow-green. They can be flocked or not, and some are trimmed with colored glass or pressed-cotton ornaments. The bases often are painted red or green. Some of the trees are tall and thin, while others are near-perfect triangles.

Today they show up at flea markets, tag sales, and antiques shows. On eBay, the on-line auction service, they are generally inexpensively priced.

Every crafted detail is perfect in this Santa created by Betty Lou Byrnes.

Sharing their amazing art that comes from their souls, these Santa artists make our lives richer at Christmastime and always.

MASTER CRAFTERS

A TOUCH OF Holly

EVERY PART OF THIS CHRISTMAS-LOVING LADY IS SPECIAL—ESPECIALLY HER LOVE OF SANTA.

Opposite and Above: *Santa sits in a sleigh filled with life-size toys and holds a working lantern.*

Perhaps Holly Howe's love of all things Christmas was destined in the stars. After all, she was supposed to be born on Christmas Day (but waited until January 3), her first name is Holly, and her middle name is Joy. It just seems a natural.

Other artistic expressions came before her passion of making Santa Claus art dolls, however. She and her husband Keith, award-winning photographers, have shared work in a portrait studio in North Platte, Nebraska, for more than 25 years. They also have raised two sons, along with the busy activities that entails.

But a few years back, Holly was mesmerized by magazine and book photography and stories of artists who created Santa figures. "To be honest, I just coveted them so much," she says. She started experimenting and created some primitive-looking figures. "My mother calls those my kindergarten Santas."

Written by Carol McGarvey ✦ *Photographs by Bill Hopkins*

Opposite: *Almost looking like real friends, Holly's pieces are large and true to life.* Above, top: *This piece titled Vincent is one of Holly's favorites.*

Holly has been greatly influenced by designers like Judith Klawitter (see story on page 82), whom she visited in Montana to take classes and workshops.

"Making the Santas represented the possibility that dreams can come true and magic can happen. I didn't know if I could do this or not, because I was so fearful. I kept telling my older son that he had to try things, that the failure was in not trying," she explains. "I realized I better be a good example for him. I shouldn't encourage him if I wasn't willing to put myself on the line too."

Her resolve and her philosophy kept her going in the Santa-crafting field. "People don't try things, because they are afraid of ridicule. I decided it wouldn't be too difficult for me to roll a ball of foil and cover it with clay. After that, it was important not to get scared by the big picture. Just take it a step at a time."

And she was off and running. Holly's expressive characters have engaging faces, each different and fitting their purpose. There's a lot of crossover, she says, between the photography and the Santas. She knows how to tilt the head "just so" to get the right look and how to put a playful glint in the eyes.

Opposite: *Grandfather Frost pulls a white swan.* Below: *Holly takes time to pick the perfect trim.* Right: *Santa dressed in a burgandy robe holds a letter from a child.*

For Holly, the hardest part of making Santa figures is working through the idea in her head, based on the materials in her stash. "It's always a compromise somewhere, but that's part of the puzzle," she says.

Her figures generally are 30 to 34 inches tall. She is always on the lookout for fabrics, trims, and accessories for her pieces. "I just love stuff and I must have a hoarding instinct. My philosophy is 'more is more,' and the more stuff I have around me to choose from, the better I feel." Holly works in an art studio in the lower level of her home, where she enjoys walking away and being able to leave the mess until she returns.

She credits husband Keith with being her cheerleader. "He's too good to me. Once we were at a doll show, and I saw some silk Swiss brocade, which was gorgeous, but it was $120 a yard so I walked away. Later Keith presented me with some of the fabric, which was wonderful."

Holly's work style is to complete each figure from start to finish focusing on one project at a time. "There's no way that I could be working on more than one at a time. My studio is such a mess after working with one Santa. When I'm done, I completely clean the work space, so that I can start completely fresh on a new piece."

Holly creates the heads and generally bulbous faces, and uses mohair from a variety of sources for the hair, beard, and mustache. For the bodies she purchases ready-made pieces with urethane foam over armature wire. With her busy work schedule, she would rather spend valuable time on the exterior of the piece. "However, I do always have to build up the elbows,

shoulders, and the knobby knees. That way, the clothing I make will fit and hang better," she explains.

For ideas she says she needs lots and lots of input. "I get books and magazines on rubber stamping, scrapbooking, quilting, and making paper collages. That doesn't mean that I'll necessarily try any of those, but I might pick up an idea or an inspiration that will work in making a Santa figure. Besides, I figure the more information that goes in, the more that might come out."

The designer loves it that she learns something new with each figure. Most of her figures sell by word of mouth for about $1,500. For the first time this year, she was in a juried show.

For her Grandfather Frost (page 68), all done in white, the figure is pulling a swan. Holly got the swan, which was originally a lawn ornament, at a garden shop. She added wheels to it and wanted to paint it a pearlized white to accompany Grandfather Frost. She looked and looked, and finally found the right paint, which turned out to be touch-up paint from an auto body shop.

Holly's detail is key to the overall look. With her Filling Requests scene, Santa is looking at a stack of letters from children and checking out his cupboard full of toys to see what he has to fulfill the wishes. "I agonized over every decision on that piece, and it took more than a year to complete," she says.

Look closely at the letters and you'll see that the stamps are from all over the world, just as Santa himself would receive. Holly copied the stamps and created the perforated edges, just like the real stamps.

Opposite and Below: *Golden beads, rich velvets, and unusual colors of blue and purple make this piece one of a kind.*

She also extended the lines of the postal cancellation to make it look authentic. "I hope the detail makes people come back and look for more."

Her Winter Wayfarer was a commissioned piece by a husband for his wife who appreciated Holly's work. "He wasn't sure exactly what he wanted in the piece, so I just had to guess. When he came to pick it up early in December, I asked when he would be giving the gift to his wife. He said not until Christmas."

However, he couldn't wait, and the next day, the delighted wife called Holly. "It was a win-win situation," Holly points out. "They absolutely made my Christmas. The wife was thrilled that her husband came up with the idea, and the husband was thrilled his wife was so happy. I was floating, and so were they."

An unusual piece is named Vincent, as in Van Gogh, says Holly with a giggle. "I had made sort of an ugly head and wasn't pleased, but decided to try to salvage it with sort of an ugly duckling approach. I resculpted him and rebaked him, poor guy, and then I accidentally dropped him. His nose shattered and one ear fell off."

Six months before, she likely would have discarded him. But new confidence told her to salvage him, and make a new nose. With skis, striped stockings, and a Tyrolean-style jacket with exquisite detail, he has added a new design dimension.

It's not surprising that Holly goes all out at Christmas. Last year, however, her family cut back from 14 trees to "only 10." Her family's home, built in the early 1900s, had at one time been a Catholic convent for two orders of teacher nuns and nurse nuns. The Howes bought the home in 1985 and had it moved down the street. Their photography studio is on the main floor, and they live on the second floor. By moving the home and building a new foundation, Holly got a lower level art studio.

Holly's can-do spirit not only inspired her children, it worked on her as well. A sign in her art studio sums it up: "Imagine what you'd try if you knew you wouldn't fail."

OLD WORLD APPEAL

COMBINING THEIR ARTISTIC TALENTS, DALE AND TAMARA WOODARD CREATE OLD-WORLD SANTAS WITH A EUROPEAN FLAIR.

In a high-tech world, Dale and Tamara Woodard of Tacoma, Washington, use the tools of a long-ago world—steel chisels, wooden mallets, and artistic brushes.

Their carved and painted Santa figures wear the pensive faces and Old World cloaks of European interpretations. "The thoughtful faces are because it's not easy being Santa Claus," says Tamara with a lilt in her voice.

Dale, a wood-carver, was born in California and Tamara, the watercolorist, in Ukraine. They met in Budapest, Hungary.

Dale first learned to carve in the Boy Scouts with a knife from his grandfather. "At the national Boy Scout Jamboree, I watched a carver make a neckerchief slide and I was hooked." Later, after studying at a carving school in Austria, he focused on Native American pieces and a few Santas. After the couple married, Dale promised he would carve a Santa figure for her each year. That promise turned into a joint business venture.

Left: *Dale's Cottonwood Bark Santas grace the walls of his workshop.* Opposite: *The faces on the pieces that Dale and Tamara create reflect a time gone by.*

Written by Carol McGarvey ✦ Photographs by Mike Jensen

Tamara, educated in the former Soviet Union, was classically trained in watercolor technique. However, when she first started on wood, she was fascinated. "I absolutely fell in love with painting on wood," she says. "It feels just like painting on paper." And unlike other Santa artists, the Woodards consider the face the most captivating and rewarding part.

"Faces and hands are the most expressive part of the body," Dale points out, "so it is important to concentrate on them to make sure they are right."

Their joint work starts with countless sketches by Tamara, which she brings to life with watercolor. Dale then makes a clay model. "That step is critical, because the drawing is two-dimensional, so the clay model takes into account the three-dimensional aspects," he says.

Dale then carves the pieces. The first carving of each design is called a genesis or bettiyo in Russian, which Dale interprets in Austrian Stone Pine called Zirbe Holz. In each piece is imbedded a bronze

Above: *A Gothic style ornament hangs on the tree.*
Right: *A close-up shows the detail of carving a figure.*
Opposite: *Three pieces show the steps in the Woodards' artistic process—Tamara's watercolor rendering, the clay model in the center, and the finished carved and painted figure.*

medallion. The carving step is followed by Tamara's painting. Each edition is limited to 24 figures. Original watercolors of the Santas and prints are available, too.

At this point the Woodards are not making reproductions of their work for the marketplace. "We just haven't found the right way to do that," Dale says. "We like that each one is separate, similar but not identical. I sometimes say that the figures are brothers, but not identical twins. We vary the details on purpose." The figures range from 15 to 18 inches in height.

Because they both were trained in Europe, Dale and Tamara give their work the serious look of religious figures in European art. "For sure, these do not have the jolly look of a Coca-Cola Santa," Dale states. "We

Opposite: *Each piece is original and made one at a time.* Top: *This signature medallion of the Anaveta Art Studio is imbedded into the base of each figure.* Above: *For Tamara and Dale Woodard of Tacoma, Washington, carving and painting Santa figures is a joint venture.* Right: *Russian Grandfather Frost carved in mahogany.*

may create an interpretation of a Thomas Nast Santa in the future, but that's about it."

Their figures vary from simply clothed gift-givers, as in Basket of Dreams or How Far?, to more elaborate St. Nicholas figures from Germany or Ukraine. Their only female figure represents Snegurochka, the Russian Snow Maiden. Tamara also paints cityscapes, and Dale carves Santa and Native American wooden portraits. Their Santa figures range up to about $2,000 each.

Their studio, in a separate building near their home in Tacoma, is work space for both, but not always at the same time. "We critique each other's work, and then go off and are able to do better work," Tamara says.

Sometimes helping them in their venture are their daughters Anastaceja and Yeleezaveta, six and four. "Often they are in the studio with us," says a proud papa. "They are developing a critical artistic eye, and both enjoy working in clay." The parents' business name, Anaveta Art Studio, is a combination of the girls' names.

Opposite: *Santa carvings vary from gift-givers to other historic-looking figures.* Below: *Every detail is critical in the work that the Woodards create. The importance of the detail of the hand is shown in this figure holding a colorful Russian matryoshka doll.*

Why focus on Santa figures? "That's easy," Dale explains. "It's a practical matter really. This is mostly a Christian nation with so many people celebrating Christmas. In books and magazines, we see that there are so many collectors. At a show once, a woman saw our pieces and said she had more than 300 Santas, but no St. Nicholas, so she bought one. Everyone seems to love the legend and the reality of Christmas."

Tamara agrees. "Christmas is the greatest celebration of the year. From the time you are little, it is special."

It's a concept the Woodards are passing along to their daughters, who are especially lucky to celebrate the best of both worlds. They celebrate Christmas twice, in December and in January, for the Orthodox holiday.

Opposite, Above, and Left: *Rich European color makes the work of Dale and Tamara unique. Small details carved and then painted with just the right hues are essential to making the pieces stand out as nontraditional Santas.*

WHAT A Ride WITH SANTA

INFLUENCING PEOPLE AROUND THE WORLD WITH HER AMAZING WORK, ARTIST JUDITH KLAWITTER HAS TOUCHED THE LIVES OF SANTA MAKERS AND SANTA LOVERS EVERYWHERE.

Santa Claus has taken artist Judith Klawitter on a lovely journey. From her first spirited forays into designing Santa figures in 1989, the two of them have been inseparable. Since that time they have taught many other artists and developed an international focus, from Africa to the White House and even to the Oprah Winfrey show.

"From the beginning, I always knew I'd be an artist. My dad thought I should get a 'real job,' but I knew I wanted to pursue art in some form. When I started down this path, I knew I would be able to show my father what I could do." Needless to say, she has succeeded, with her life-size figures sometimes bringing about $18,000 to $20,000.

That's a far cry from the first primitive versions she made from cornstarch and bread dough, built over a bud vase body. With husband Paul and their family, Judith had moved from her native Missoula, Montana, to Ocean Springs, Mississippi. "My work was horrible. Even though Santa is forgiving, that was not a good start. I knew there must be a better way."

After seeing an article in *Country Home* magazine in the mid-1980s, Judith was inspired to keep trying. "I

Above and Opposite: *Detail abounds and magic unfolds on every piece that Judith creates.*

Written by Carol McGarvey ✦ Photographs by Mark Bryant

really needed some inspiration," she explains. "Our family was moving every two years for Paul's job as a Navy air traffic controller, and I was becoming severely depressed. Seriously, my creativity was my lifeline." She had grown up around Western art and was adept at wood carving wildlife and figures in nature, but not people.

"Then my husband got me some doll magazines, and they opened up a whole new world for me. However, I knew I would need to create my own niche." What she decided on was to become known for wrinkles!

"I decided that a realistic approach to faces was the best way for me to go," Judith explains. "I have always been attracted to black-and-white photos of older people, because of their realism. Plus I remember my grandmother's wonderful face, which represented peace and unconditional love. Now that I'm getting my own wrinkles, however, they're becoming a bit too real."

An ordained minister, Judith believes Santa represents many of the wonderful attributes of God—a fatherly figure who is generous beyond measure. He brings peace and joy into our lives, but most of all he loves us unconditionally.

She cites one of her favorite sculptures, Babushka, the female European Santa figure. "She represents how we all become. She was cleaning her house when the three Wise Men came to her and asked directions and offered to take her with them as they searched for the Child Jesus. She said no, she was too busy. Later, when she realized what she had missed, she spent the rest of

Opposite: *A beautiful Old World Santa is rich in detail.* Above, left: *Pieces of lace and other vintage detail are used to embellish this beautiful Santa.* Above, right: *Judith has a plan for every detail and executes it perfectly. She concentrates on making the faces look real by creating the wrinkles of time.*

her life traveling around giving gifts to children, trying to find the child that she missed."

Over the years Judith's work has inspired other artists to visit her for week-long classes on techniques. "I promise them a major headache by Friday," she says. "They take so many notes, but they still need the safety net of how-to procedures. So now I offer five videotapes on my website, so they can fast forward or rewind to get a technique." She says she knows that building the body foundations and getting proportion and scale right is not fun, but it is paramount to creating a pleasing form.

Judith favors working in large-scale figures, with most being life-size. Her skill comes in the faces, and she is known for them. "I want each face different from the other. Faces are my signature. Each time before I start to sculpt, I ask God to work through me and bless my mind and hands."

Ideas for faces come in a variety of ways. A main one is from the photos in *National Geographic* magazine, because they represent people from around the world. Judith says she might look at a photo for months before deciding how to incorporate it.

That happened with a photo taken by a former student from Mississippi, who visited the Congo with her husband who was on a medical mission trip. "When I saw a photo taken on that trip of an elderly woman, I was mesmerized," Judith states. "She looked to be 70 or 80 years old, even though she likely was much younger. But her face just said 'I love you unconditionally,' and I knew that I would have to use that face somehow."

Opposite: *This beautiful Santa is named Unconditional Love.* Above: *Judith stands among her creations that become almost like family.*

Judith was so moved by the needs of the African people that she considered going there herself. "However, I am hard of hearing, and I figured that I would be in the way on such a trip." What she did do, however, was to interpret the face of the woman in the photo into a black Santa wearing long white robes. (See page 86.) Judith heard that Oprah Winfrey had gone to Africa and would be raising funds to help the country's children through her Angel Network. Judith is donating her black Santa titled Unconditional Love to the Angel Network. "Perhaps I can't go to Africa myself, but this Santa and I will help make a difference. It's how I can do my part."

Every year Judith makes four or five figures. She decides to do a piece de resistance, even if it means bending rules and breaking the mold. "I want people to stop and look." She may mull over an idea for months, thinking and plotting and looking for the "just right" details. "For my figures, it is so important that I do a lot of historical research. Then I go from there in the planning. Truly, truly, I can hyperventilate over a piece of fabric or a little toy for an accessory." She might have two or three weeks of sculptural work, but she might have thought about a figure for six years. That's the case with a cowboy figure she's been working on.

Besides her classes and instructional videos, Judith writes a column in *Doll Crafter* magazine, which increases her national base. "I really try to enable people to use and to develop their God-given talents and abilities."

Celebrities such as Demi Moore and former President Bill Clinton and Senator Hilary Clinton own pieces of her work. Her work called All God's

Opposite and Above: *Judith's Santa grouping called All God's Creatures is in a private collection in California.*

Creatures, pages 88 and 89, which shows a woodlands-style Santa working with animals, went to Dr. Laura Pasten of Carmel, California, a veterinarian to Hollywood celebrities. Museums around the world also showcase Judith's pieces.

Judith also helps other artists who live in rural areas and may not have access to supplies. On her website, www.jklawitter.com, she has a link to Agape Supply, which offers wool, glass eyes, components for forming doll bodies, and tools.

This year Judith took Santa on a ride too. She and Paul moved near Coeur d'Alene, Idaho, to be closer to children and grandchildren. The process forced her to organize her "bazillion" Santa-making supplies into plastic bins. "While my new studio will be a huge space over an extra-large garage, Santa artists know that in reality, they take over the whole house."

For Judith and Santa, it's a win-win situation. "We're having too much fun!"

Opposite, Above, and Left: *Judith's life-size Santas appear very real as they appear in outdoor settings.*

A Very Mary Christmas

SANTA IS JUST A PART OF MARY ENGELBREIT'S NATURE—AND SHE TEACHES US ALL TO BELIEVE.

Author Clement C. Moore and artist Mary Engelbreit never met, of course. But 180-some years after he penned the enchanting story of Santa's ride in *The Night Before Christmas,* she repackaged it in color and whimsy and gave it to children of all ages.

The story goes that in 1822, Moore, a biblical scholar and literature professor at the Episcopal seminaries of New York City, combined images and stories into a delightful tale as a gift for his six children, which has become a classic.

In 2004, it was a natural that Mary, who had been drawing roly-poly Santa figures for many years, should publish her own artful interpretation of the classic tale (HarperCollins). Because of today's technology, she was able to share her version in the DVD format as well, to the delight of an even larger audience of children (Schwartz & Associates).

Above: *Mary works in her St. Louis studio.* Left: *Mary has depicted The Night Before Christmas in a charming book and DVD in her delightful style.* Opposite: *One of Mary's many charming Santa cards.*

Written by Carol McGarvey ✦ Photographs by Ron Klein

SANTA

"It is such a classic poem," says the prolific artist, who estimates she has drawn more than 4,000 illustrations in her professional career. "It's the story we all know, and the one most of us can recite word for word."

She knows that for many people, childhood memories are linked to Christmastime. "That's certainly true in my own case. We had such wonderful Christmases when I was little. We visited Santa at a downtown department store with its colorful decorated windows. It was magic. There were no malls then. We would visit 'Toyland' and then go out to dinner. It was such an annual tradition," she remembers. "There was no reason to change a thing from year to year."

And Christmas, of course, was a frame of mind and a length of time. "I love everything about the Christmas season," she wrote in one of her books. "It is definitely a season—one day a year would never be enough."

Christmas is a feast of the senses, she feels. "I love the first glimpse of 'old friend' ornaments as they're unearthed from the box in the back of the closet, the pine forest smell of the freshly cut tree that these cherished decorations will soon transform, and the comforting sound of a holiday hymn being sung by an enthusiastic, if not pitch-perfect, group of carolers."

A couple of Mary's Santa Claus illustrations are known as the "Believe Santas." With that simple word,

Above and Opposite: *Santa with children, on a reindeer, gardening, or on the beach—Mary always portrays him as the Jolly Old Elf.*

ME
THE CHRISTMAS GARDEN

S.S. CLAUS
ME

she encourages remembering simpler times, quieter times, and all that the word may conjure up to various individuals. "That all started with my own kids. They kept wondering how such a big guy would get down our chimney. I just kept encouraging them to believe it could and would happen." The word can apply to so many situations, she explains.

In *The Night Before Christmas* book, the St. Louis, Missouri, artist relishes in details, in her inimitable style—decorated dormers and eyebrow windows, candles and garlands, swags and quilts, flowers and fancy treats. In this book and other pieces, Mary's Santa characters usually are dressed in the Old World style with a long cloak. Her comforting illustrations draw on the wonders of the holiday season in their messages—"To a Friend's House the Road Is Never Long," "Let Innocence and Joy Prevail," "The More the Merrier" (about cookies, of course), and "Claus and Effect." Along the way are one-word depictions—Hope, Harmony, Faith, and Believe.

In one depiction, a relaxed Santa in casual attire asks, "Is Christmas Fun or What?"

All is not lost on tinsel, lights, food, and presents. Mary depicts the annual Christmas pageant, peace on earth, glad tidings, and the Nativity, in "Day of Light, Day of Birth, Here Is God Come to Earth."

Mary's myriad licensing program showcases her work

Opposite: *The elaboration on Santa's coat is repeated in the border of this favorite Santa card.* Above: *No one does "Believe" better than Mary. She makes Santa come to life.*

LET THE MERRYMAKING BEGIN!
THE LIST
ME

in items from stationery, pottery, fabric, greeting cards for all occasions, scrapbooking items, and paper towels. One new venture is resin Santa Claus figures in her classic style, to be marketed through the Bradford Exchange.

In hustle-bustle times with e-mail and instant messaging, Mary sees a need for greeting cards, especially at Christmastime. "We love that our cards have become a tradition for many families. We don't want to lose longtime contact with our friends, so sending cards, even though it is time-consuming, is especially important."

Opposite: *Mary's cards are full of detail with happiness throughout.* Above: *Mary's greeting card line continues to be successful as buyers come back year after year choosing her cards to send and give.*

Her magazine staff at *Mary Engelbreit's HOME COMPANION* works hard to come up with interesting features, especially for the holiday issue. "While people treasure their long-time holiday traditions, they also want to see new spins on how to interpret that in their homes."

Mary's work is geared to making people happy, she says. "I want people to go into our store in St. Louis, for example, and feel better. I love to imagine how women in particular will interpret our ideas and how they will use them in their lives."

What's next? "There are so many areas we have dipped our toes into, and we'd like to explore them more. I loved doing the Santa Claus DVD, so we're developing more animation and children's projects." Mary's illustrations of *100 Mother Goose Rhymes* is

ME

coming out soon, followed by *Nursery Tales*, a collection of 15 stories.

The artist describes her detailed style as old-fashioned and comforting. She also has dipped her pen into the Arts and Crafts style and has introduced several products in that mode. "The Arts and Crafts period always has inspired me, and I try to incorporate it often into my work. I like to point out that not everything has changed in our world."

Now that Mary is a grandmother to granddaughter Mikayla, Christmas has become even more magical. "It's just like starting all over again," she exclaims. "I have an entire basement of Christmas decorations, and my kids thought I had to put out every single item each year, because they would remember them. With a grandchild, however, it's a new slate. She doesn't remember some of those old items, so it can be a simpler approach."

Opposite and Above: *Sometimes Santa has a round face and sometimes a silly face, but always a face that says "Merry Christmas!"*

The artist enjoys decorating her own home with works of other artists and a collection of vintage ornaments and decorations.

But for the artist, some things have not changed. For example, she has not put Santa Claus on a diet. He's still roly-poly and wears bottlecap glasses.

You'll notice too, that Santa is not exactly politically correct in Mary's interpretation. He still smokes a pipe in many of her pieces.

"Hey, that's his problem," says the artist with a chuckle.

From the Heart Art

ALWAYS ON THE LOOKOUT FOR THE NEXT FOUND OBJECT THAT WILL MAKE HER ART, LEE MIDDLESWART BRINGS LIFE AND HEART INTO HER CHRISTMAS FOLK ART.

Lee Middleswart of Indianola, Iowa, uses found objects, antique pieces, and collectibles in fashioning her Santa Clauses, angels, and other art. But she also includes a priceless ingredient in each one—a piece of her heart.

Pretty much self-taught, Lee used to embellish items as strange as garbage trucks during her days as a commercial artist. Without a doubt, creating her folk art figures is much more fun. But her passage from commercial artist to folk artist came in a most unexpected way when the loss of her younger son triggered a deep depression.

"I saw life as more fragile and challenging and these qualities changed the way I made art," she explains. There really is healing in art therapy, and it was a driving force behind Lee's reclaiming her life.

Perhaps quite naturally, she started creating angels as a symbolic link to her son and she often gave them to others who also were in pain. A shop owner in a nearby city asked to sell the angels in her store, and a host of custom orders followed. "I simply couldn't believe that people really liked my work," says Lee. But they did, and they do, and her work has mushroomed, as has her confidence.

Left: *A trio of angels stands ready to perform a Christmas song.* Opposite: *Santas by the dozens fill Lee's home and bring smiles to everyone who sees them.*

Written by Carol McGarvey ✦ Photographs by Jay Wilde

A counselor encouraged her to branch out with her whimsical designs and to explore the national world of folk art. "They encouraged me to visit a folk art society convention in Milwaukee, Wisconsin, to explore the work of others. Needless to say, I was so surprised to discover that my therapy art was actually folk art. I felt like I had finally found my niche."

At one point, two sales representatives from the Folk Fest in Atlanta, Georgia, contacted her and she created three pieces each month to sell through them. Now her work has a national audience. She creates pieces for various collectors around the country.

Lee does it all, from carving, woodburning, and sanding, to painting, and staining. Her workshop is organized with bins and containers full of trims, embellishments, wires, beads, fabrics, and architectural details. Nearby is the meticulous woodworking workshop of husband Gary. "He has taught me how to use his tools, and he helps me as needed."

The two plan vacations and weekend jaunts around flea markets and antiques shows. "I'm so lucky that we enjoy this pastime together," Lee says. "We really delight in finding something that would work well on the folk art figures. We truly have lots of fun doing this together, whether it's shopping, browsing, or gathering interesting pieces of driftwood or architectural details." If she can't find the right piece for a project in her driftwood stash, she'll often start with a commercial post or rail from a home center.

An old baking powder tin or a wooden cigar box might turn into the torso for a figure; a conch shell might become a Santa head; or a wooden spoon might

Above, left: *An old can becomes Santa's red suit.* Left: *Painting the piece is just part of Lee's work.* Opposite, above: *Lee collects all kinds of flea market finds to use in her art and keeps them in bins in her studio.* Opposite, below: *Lee's Santas come in various shapes and sizes and are made from all kinds of materials.*

Opposite and Above: *Some of Lee's Santas are large and come dressed in fur. This one is about 36 inches tall.* Above, right: *Lee also makes other Christmas pieces such as this grouping of Joseph, Mary, and baby Jesus.*

become the base for the painted faces on Mary and Joseph in Nativity figures made from driftwood. Old leather gloves might be recycled into black boots on a Santa character.

A single, old-fashioned large light bulb might become a decoration around the neck of a woodland-style Santa, or a piece of an old quilt might see new duty as a cloak for a European-looking Santa.

Friends, too, get in on the act. They have been known to swoop up interesting items in parking lots to give to Lee for her figures. "The ideas are limitless," says Lee. "There is always a use for something."

Originally from California, Lee came to Iowa as a single mother with her two young sons and found a home in the Midwest. She took some commercial art classes at a local college to get started in the area that would give her new life.

the dream goes on

Opposite: *Lee created a Santa with a Christmas tree tummy that really lights up.* Left: *Lee Middleswart creates her one-of-a-kind art from her charming studio.* Below: *A compass shows the way on this folk art Santa.*

Lee's process for creating her whimsical Santa Clauses and other figures often starts while she's sleeping. "I see the Santa in my mind, almost as a spiritual connection and a slide show presentation. It is a little like being tied to an umbilical cord," she explains. "As I'm working on a piece, I must bring the components of the figure into my bedroom. Then I know I'll think about it during the night."

Lee thrives on the details of the process. Faces set the mood for a piece, and Lee has several faces she works with, often starting with the "just right" nose. The rest of the face naturally follows, it seems, no matter if she is using sculpting clay or paper clay. Simple acrylic paints add rich color.

Lee says taking a close look at the world around her inspires her. Once on an elevator she saw a little boy holding a plastic bag full of water and goldfish. That inspired her to create a mixed media folk art picture of that scene. Another time, working on designs for a nearby Underground Railroad museum inspired a series of black figures, because she felt empathy with their plight during the Civil War.

A whirligig with movable arms she created several years ago tells her own poignant story beautifully:

"I do believe
The world is beautiful
And some day
I will get out of bed
And fly."

And she has.

THE Eyes HAVE IT

LOOK INTO THE EYES OF ANY OF BETTY LOU'S SANTAS AND YOU WILL KNOW YOU JUST MET THE REAL ST. NICK.

Santa Claus and Betty Lou Byrnes of Naperville, Illinois, have had a "thing" going for years. "He always has held a special place in my heart," says the art doll maker who specializes in Santa characters. "I consider each one of my handcrafted Santas a labor of love."

She had to work—and suffer—a bit before finding the right medium for her artistic expression. In 1999,

Left: *Betty Lou started creating Santas in wood until she realized it was too dangerous for her.* Above and Opposite: *All dressed in white, this beautiful piece stands about two feet tall.*

Written by Carol McGarvey ✦ *Photographs by Andy Lyons*

Betty Lou started wood carving, which she found fascinating. "The best advice, of course, is to always carve away from your body. Well, that just meant that I would cut my legs," she explains in an embarrassed tone. "I was always going to the emergency room and constantly had stitches and butterfly patches."

However, her life changed when she saw a *Better Homes and Gardens, Santa Claus Collection* book and became enamored by the work of Judith Klawitter (see page 82). Needless to say, working with polymer clay and fabric seemed a bit less dangerous than carving tools, she says with a giggle.

So in 2000, her husband Don drove her to Montana through the smoke of forest fires to take a class from Judith. Her rise in the doll world has been a bit meteoric. By 2002, Betty Lou was one of 12 students selected by Jack Johnston, founder of the Professional Doll Makers Art Guild, to take his professional class in Salt Lake City, Utah. During the following two years, her Nutcracker Santa was featured in *Contemporary Doll Collector* magazine, and Father Winter and Santa

Opposite, Above, and Below: *The artistic detail on Betty Lou's Santas is something she is proud of and strives to improve all the time.*

Opposite, Above, and Right: *Betty Lou uses purchased toys and trims on her pieces. This Santa carries a cone filled with goodies and treats.*

Building a Train appeared in *Doll Crafter Magazine.*

"I always loved art and doing things with my hands," says the former advertising pasteup artist. She and Don moved around during his Air Force days and his time as an airline pilot, and art was something she could take with her. Art also gave her flexibility while raising two sons. Now, with seven grandchildren, she has a whole new Santa audience.

"Christmas is so special," Betty Lou says. "Ask anyone. I am known for decking the halls and then some. If there's a nook or a cranny, I put up some holiday decoration." She doesn't just make Santa; she collects

too. Her collection probably numbers more than 200, because "each one spoke to me." They are made of wood, clay, or fabric, or they are reproductions.

For her art doll pieces, she uses polymer sculpting clay to create the head, hands, and feet of her figures, giving each Santa the warm, natural expression he deserves. Fine glass eyes add the "twinkle factor." Soft mohair provides a finished look with snowy white hair and flowing beard. Depending on the size—about 15 inches for the smallest, and about 33 for the largest—she makes a wire armature, then forms a soft-sculpture body.

"Since clothes make the man, I spend lots of time adding special trims, along with itty-bitty treasures and toys."

Betty Lou works from start to finish on each Santa, finishing one before starting another. Generally she spends three to four weeks on each one.

Her rich Father Winter figure is a vision in white, embellished with fur and subtle trims. As a contrast, her Victorian Santa is wearing elegant robes, a ruffle-front shirt and a holly wreath on his head. A favorite, Silent Night, with Santa's index finger to his mouth to "shhhhh" a schnauzer, while Santa arranges gifts under

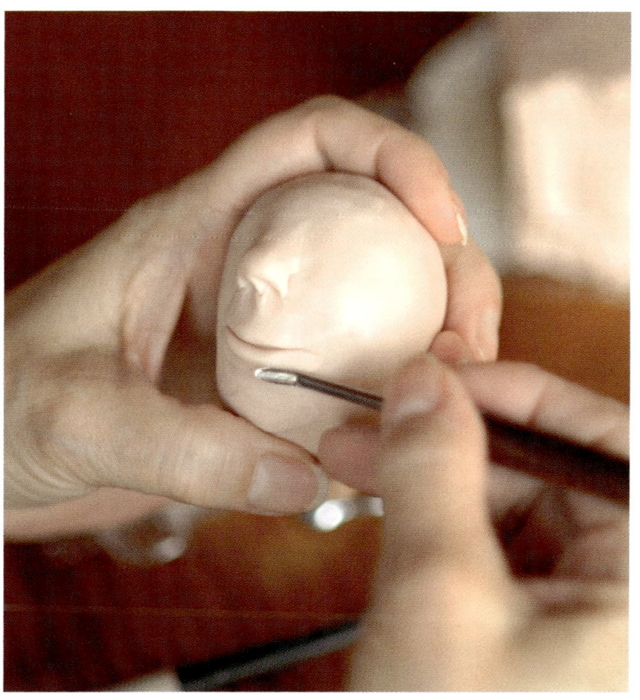

Opposite and Left: *Santa tries to keep the little dog quiet while he brings the gifts.* Above: *Betty Lou uses a polymer clay to sculpt the heads.*

a tree, is based on a family pet named Gretchen. Betty Lou sculpted the dog for the scene.

On another special one, Santa Building a Train, Betty Lou honored husband Don's model train hobby with a Santa in a railroader's hat (see page 120). One figure, called Downhill Racer, below, has Santa whooshing down a hill on a Flexible Flyer sled, holding onto his colorful stocking cap. She's also very proud of one original doll, a riverboat captain, named Speedy Steamboat Sam, designed by school children to honor the Grand Excursion, a boat celebration in Illinois.

Above: *Betty Lou and husband, Don, enjoy their Santa friends in their log home in Illinois.* Left, Above, and Opposite: *Many of the figures that Betty Lou makes have an elfish appearance that makes every onlooker smile.*

Left and Below: *Husband Don collects model trains and Betty Lou provides a Santa just for him.* Opposite: *All of the Santas that Betty Lou makes seem like they are filled with the spirit of Christmas.*

That piece is now part of an exhibit in the Galena Historical Museum.

Betty Lou creates about 10 Santa figures each year. They sell in Galena shops and galleries and in trade and doll shows, generally for $500 to $1,000 each.

"I'm always on the lookout for old fabrics, including velvets and wools, along with toys and other trims," she says. She orders fur from a Montana rancher. Don often helps with the technical parts and the bases. For the stand-up pieces, there's a metal rod in the base, along with hollow rods in the figures' legs, which interlock for standing, but come apart for shipping.

"With each one, I feel as if I've given birth," says the art doll artist. "Yes, it's hard to let go of them. I have to know that they're going to good homes."

With her proceeds, of course, she purchases new materials and starts spreading the joy—and the twinkle of the eyes—all over again.

The Folk Art Factor

JIM SHORE'S USE OF EXQUISITE DETAIL AND QUILTLIKE EMBELLISHMENTS MAKE HIS SANTAS ONE-OF-A-KIND WORKS OF ART.

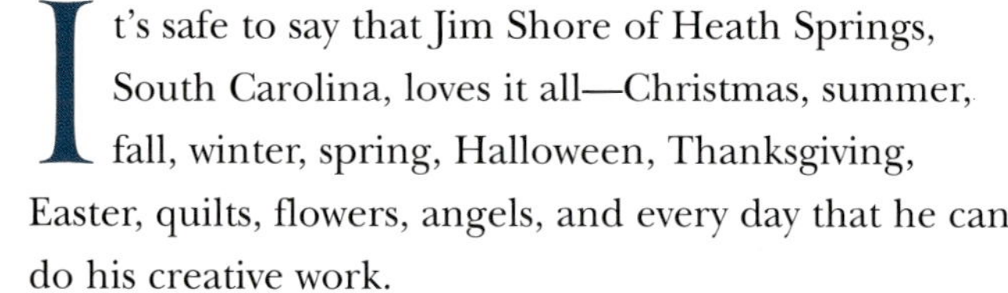

It's safe to say that Jim Shore of Heath Springs, South Carolina, loves it all—Christmas, summer, fall, winter, spring, Halloween, Thanksgiving, Easter, quilts, flowers, angels, and every day that he can do his creative work.

The work of this prolific artist and wood carver has become a favorite of many around the world for its exuberance and bright colors. Since 2002, he has gathered new fans with his Heartwood Creek line, licensed by Enesco in gift shops and fabric and quilt shops.

Jim was trained as an engineer, but couldn't ignore the call to his artistic roots. "My parents were creative people, and growing up in South Carolina, we kids were expected to perfect different projects and techniques, such as stained glass, gold-smithing, making furniture, and painting portraits."

Jim says he loves the precision of his detailed pieces and the realism that he can incorporate in them. From numerous Santa figures with colorfully

Left: *Santa, dressed in a robe embellished wih colorful birdhouses, cradles his feathered friends.* Opposite: *With detail like the great masters of long ago, these Santas display their art on their suits and accessories.*

Written by Carol McGarvey ✦ Photographs by Andy Lyons
Photographed at Tangen House, Living History Farms, Urbandale, IA

Opposite: *The scale of this large Santa makes it a wonderful piece to display on the floor in any room of the house.* Below: *The pencil Santa displays bold color and exquisite detail on the cape and body of the tall and slender piece.* Below, right: *Jim Shore sits among his amazing pieces of art.*

embellished cloaks and prancing reindeer to whimsical cats and enchanting Noah's Ark figures, he has a hard time keeping up with the ideas he keeps having. "Truly, I make lists of the lists I need to make," he says with a laugh.

In the early 1990s Jim is credited with making the first so-called "pencil Santa" figures with his own company before joining Enesco. "There were so many Santas on the market. It just seemed as if there needed to be a different look. I honestly didn't know if a tall, skinny Santa would be accepted. But they sold like hotcakes. It was great fun!"

Look closely at Jim's work, and you'll see lots of bright colors—purple, red, deep blue, and shocking pink. "I love color-play. It's challenging and rewarding,

and, you know what? I love ignoring standard color rules and adding a surprise punch of bright color where it's not expected. When it comes to color, I run the gamut, from pastels to deep, bold Amish solid colors. Just for fun, I throw in hot orange or bright turquoise."

The artist credits a little luck and a lot of serendipity to his success. He also appreciates the role of the past as he interprets his pieces. For example, each piece incorporates quilt patterns. "The quilt patterns are the anchor of my work. I love the research, because I'm such an admirer of quilt history," he explains. "Quilting is one of the true art forms in America, and it is so underappreciated. These women very simply needed blankets for their families, but they used a high level of artistic brilliance to make those blankets." He and his wife Jan have a "small" collection, he says, of about 130 quilts.

Opposite: *Whether on the front or on the back of Jim's Santas, quilt patterns are always a key element in his designs.* Above: *Jim uses the front of Santa's robe to display scenes of the countryside in bold colors.* Left: *Even Santa's sailboat is decorated with beautiful embellishments and color.*

The Santa Claus figures and the Christmas items are among Jim's favorites. "When I went with Enesco, one of the vice presidents suggested that I do something a little different, and that's really when the folk art came into play. I decided to incorporate a primitive look, adding in floral techniques like rosemaling, Norwegian rose painting, and hindeloopen, a Dutch floral style."

For his Heartwood Creek line, Jim creates about 150 to 180 seasonal pieces a year. One piece spawns myriad ideas for many others. He carves original pieces from basswood or tupelo wood and sculpts with doll makers' clay for detail work.

He's in the process of building a new studio, but most of the time he works all over the house, from the sunroom to the kitchen counter.

Jim has a steadfast philosophy about his work. It indicates why he licenses his work and does not create

Opposite and Above: *Jim carves pieces that coordinate with Santa such as reindeer and sleighs with the same exquisite detail.*

Opposite: *Santa cuddles a kitty in this charming piece carved for cat and Christmas lovers everywehre.* Left: *This beautiful Santa figure is called God's Blessings are Forever.*

limited editions. "I want anyone who sees the Santas and other figures to be able to buy them. I wouldn't want to hear that someone loved something, but then couldn't enjoy it because of money reasons."

Recently he took on a new task, one he considers a coup. Jim is collaborating with Disney. "I will interpret Disney pieces in Jim Shore style, which should be great fun. The first line is a patriotic one and includes Minnie Mouse as Betsy Ross, and other fun pieces. It will be like art within the art." He's also working on the Princess line, with Sleeping Beauty and Snow White.

Christmas at the Shore's home is festive, because "Jan is a Christmas fanatic," says a proud husband. "She has thousands of ornaments, from dime store varieties to serious pieces. We put up five trees to showcase them. Between us, we have six children and four grandchildren, so the holidays are great fun."

Jim has a rule at Christmas. "I don't care how old you are, you must believe. If you don't believe, then Santa Claus won't bring any presents."

Pieces of the Past

USING TINY SCRAPS AND BITS OF PRECIOUS FINDS, JEAN LITTLEJOHN CREATES SANTAS THAT HAVE PERSONALITY-PLUS.

Growing up in the Appalachian Mountains during the Great Depression of the 1930s, Jean Littlejohn of Clyde, North Carolina, learned how to "make do."

"We had nothing, but neither did anyone else," she says. "My mother would turn old coats inside out and make new jackets for us, and she would take apart knitted items and teach us how to make new things. I learned how to knit and purl and to tat with a shuttle by age five." She learned to crochet, and also made her own clothes by age 12 with a treadle sewing machine.

Her mother, a perfectionist, made Jean tear out knitting or sewing projects if they weren't just right and start over. "She taught us well, and we learned how to do things right."

It may sound grim, but Jean doesn't remember it that way at all. "We had a happy house, and we always had so much fun at Christmas, making paper chains and finding candies in our father's socks. I remember getting a doll—I still have it—that Mother made a white batiste dress for, and she trimmed it with tatted roses. We were the original recyclers."

Today Jean stitches all those memories into her Northwoods Santa figures that she makes to sell. From just a few inches to six feet tall, and from a few dollars to $2,500, her work is cherished by shoppers and collectors who come back for more.

Jean has a knack for scouring flea markets, thrift shops, and antiques stores in her never-ending quest for buttons, lace, old quilt tops, furs,

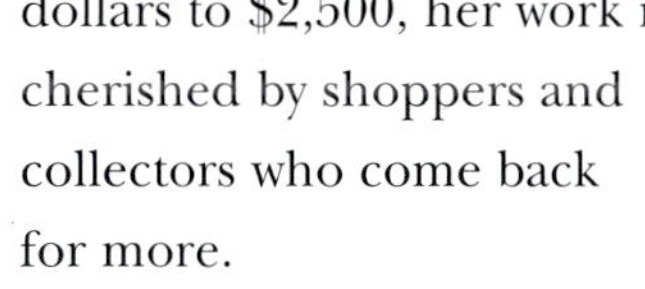

Opposite: *A patriotic Santa sits among tiny trims in his handmade sleigh.* Right: *Santa rests in a sleigh filled with tiny treasures.*

Written by Carol McGarvey ✦ *Photographs by Bill Hopkins*

and costume jewelry. Every spring she goes to a big street sale in Lancaster County, Pennsylvania, where she always finds treasures.

In the 1960s, Jean started making dolls and was invited to a juried show at the Village of Yesteryear in Raleigh. "I made Raggedy Ann and Andy dolls, dried apple dolls, and a number of Mr. and Mrs. Claus figures. At that time, the Santa dolls didn't attract too many buyers. A few years later, however, the Santa dolls seemed to catch on," she recalls.

The next year she doubled her Santa doll quota and just kept on adding to her growing demand. Her figures range from 10 to 12 inches up to 36 and 42 inches. She makes some standing and some sitting characters.

Above: *Heads and bodies wait to become Santas.* Left: *Jean's Santas sit by the dozens in her Christmas studio.* Opposite: *Santas come in all sizes and shapes in Jean's Santa imagination.*

Jean uses a combination of materials, from oven-baked clay to wooden bodies. Over time, she has developed her own special recipe for papier-mâché. Husband David helps with the wood parts and fashions an occasional curlicue sleigh for Santa to sit in.

"The hardest part is the face," says the artist. "Getting the face right can be tough, and the nose and eyes must be just right." She uses acrylic paint to get the coloring correct. She uses wood and heavy-gauge wire for the body armatures. Achieving the right proportion for the sitting ones is especially critical.

Jean works on the faces during the winter in a mass-production format, creating up to 100 for the next season. Then the faces can dry near the heat registers. After that, however, each Santa is completed one at a time. Each is a different size and gets a separate pattern for the clothes, depending on the materials Jean decides to use on it. To fill out the bodies, she wraps the body structures with fiberfill

Below: *Jean uses a variety of materials to create her one-of-a-kind Santas.* Opposite: *Jean's Santas are rich in detail using various tiny trims.*

and fabric strips. David often carves wooden shoes or leather boots for the figures.

Using a sewing machine and hand sewing, she creates the garment, which varies by the fabric she chooses. For the beards, she uses angora, llama, or alpaca wool. "People think I order that and it comes in a bag. Oh, how I wish!" Instead, she collects the dirty wool from a friend who raises sheep, and it must be washed and dried. She has found someone else with Cotswold sheep and she enjoys using the curly wool. Another messy part is treating the wool for moths. Sometimes on the figures, Jean sprinkles the wool with mica flakes for a frosty look.

Jean's favorite part is embellishing each Santa with fringe, beads, tiny boxes, and miniature toys. For dolls in Santa's pack, she uses a mold constructed from an antique "frozen Charlotte" doll from Japan. The small dolls are molded from porcelain, and Jean paints and

fires them as needed. She makes the details from modeling clay.

Jean's Father Christmas figures have been in the national spotlight. The famous Biltmore Estate in nearby Asheville, North Carolina, commissioned her work for seven years at its gift house. And one holiday season, her work was featured on the mantel on the holiday set of ABC's *Good Morning America.* As a result she even got an order from Saudi Arabia for a piece of her work. She has created various six-foot Santas for hotels to display in their lobbies during the holidays.

Her community looks forward to her annual Northwoods Santa Shoppe, open from the day after Thanksgiving until the day before Christmas. For 25 years, the shop was in her home. But when she and David moved to a nearby town, there was not easy access to her home, so the shop is in a friend's house a mile from Jean's home. For repeat collectors she often e-mails a digital photo of new items.

Why is Christmas so special for Jean? "I am a child at heart, and that will never change."

Opposite: *Heads of all sizes and shapes wait to become part of Jean's collection.* Above, top: *Jean creates a variety of looks in her dolls.* Above: *Jean sits with one of her favorite Santas in her Santa-making studio.*

A Story for the Children

SUZI SMITH USES HER DOLLS TO SHARE THE STORY OF SANTA CLAUS BRINGING GREAT JOY TO BELIEVERS OF ALL AGES.

It seems only natural that, at some point, Suzi Smith of Candler, North Carolina, would combine two of her loves— doll-making and Christmas.

"I was a tomboy when I was growing up," Suzi explains, "but you know what? I still loved dolls. They have stuck with me my whole life." She started taking doll classes in 1981, after dabbling in many other crafts. Her specialty has become porcelain-head dolls.

From the initial painting on greenware doll heads and firing them in the kiln to creating the characters and sewing the clothing—definitely not her favorite part of the process—Suzi enjoys watching the dolls' personalities emerge.

She savors the hunt for adding to her stash of vintage clothing, fabric, old furs, trims, or costume jewelry. She will adapt nearly anything. A case in point involves a long-ago family trip to Pennsylvania. "We saw a beautiful dead pheasant in the road. I made my husband Bruce pull over so that we could collect some of the gorgeous feathers. About 15 years later, I used those feathers in creating very interesting wings for a snow angel doll that I entered in a prestigious international competition," Suzi explains. "That doll won third place, and I just know it had to do with her unusual wings."

Her doll commissions have gone to families and to celebrities. One family wanted 12 baby dolls. "Fortunately, I didn't have to dress them," says the reluctant seamstress with a chuckle. "The grandmother wanted to dress the dolls, which was great with me!"

In 1985, a commissioned doll went to country entertainer Barbara Mandrell. In 1988, a character doll depicting Dr. C. Everett Koop, former surgeon general of the United States, was presented to him at his retirement dinner.

When she started making Santa Claus dolls, Suzi researched the history of the gift-giving figure in many countries. "When I make the Santa dolls, I start with an

Written by Carol McGarvey ✦ Photographs by Bill Hopkins

idea, such as a photo in a book or a holiday card. I let the doll evolve, often depending on the fabric and trims I have collected."

Suzi enjoys giving programs about doll-making to various groups. So when her older daughter Teresa, a special education teacher, worked on a project with her fifth-graders, she asked her mother to become involved. Students were to research various countries and give written and oral reports. At the grand finale of the project, parents, faculty, and friends came to hear the reports and to learn about the students' research.

Suzi presented her story of the evolution of Santa Claus, from country to country, showing her dolls to represent the various Santa figures throughout history. To tell the story, she uses mostly her own handmade dolls, often fashioned from wire armatures and cloth bodies, embellished with mohair fur, satin, gold lamé, velvet, tulle, wool, lace, and rickrack. "When Teresa thought there should somehow be a female Santa figure, I went right to my unfinished dolls and created a LaBefana doll from Italy," Suzi notes.

From St. Nicholas and Père Noel to Kris Kringle and the current Santa Claus, Suzi shares the history. She always ends with figures showing the Nativity, to emphasize the real meaning of Christmas.

"Everyone loves the story of Santa, because Christmas is such a special time of year," Suzi says. "No doubt, it's my favorite time, because we are able to celebrate the traditions passed down in our families. Leaving cookies out for Santa, hanging ornaments on the tree, and preparing a large family dinner on Christmas Eve are all special to me. It's a special time, because people are in such a good mood."

Above, left: *Suzi created a Belsnickle as part of her story for the children.* Above: *Suzi relaxes with her Santas that she uses to tell the story to special children everywhere.*

Suzi Smith's Visual Story of Santa

The story begins with ST. NICHOLAS, an actual person born in A.D. 280 in a city in Asia Minor, now Turkey. He became an ordained Roman Catholic bishop at the young age of 19, the youngest bishop in the history of the church. Later in life, after inheriting his wealthy merchant father's riches, Nicholas used his wealth to help people in need. He constantly gave gifts to orphans, widows, and poor people, and became known as the Supreme Gift Giver. A modest man, he didn't like to be seen when he delivered presents. So he often told children to go to sleep quickly so they would not see him bringing their gifts.

One story of his generosity involves rescuing three young sisters from a bad situation. It was the custom for girls to marry young, but each was required to have a suitable dowry, or large portion of money, to give to her husband-to-be. The oldest daughter was soon to be married, but her poor father had no money for her dowry. Nicholas heard of her predicament and dropped bags of gold into the stockings the girl had left hanging to dry by the fire.

St. Nicholas

His good works inspired more people of Myra to join the Christian Church, even though in A.D. 303, the Roman emperor commanded all citizens to worship him as a god. Christians who believed in only one God could not, in good conscience, obey him. The emperor threatened their stubbornness with torture and imprisonment. Nicholas himself spent five years in a cold, dark prison. After his death, the people told tales of his kindness and credited him with miracles. Soon people started calling him a saint.

The story of SANTA CLAUS in America begins with the Dutch settlements in the colony of New York. When the Dutch landed in what is now Manhattan on Christmas Day in 1624, they named St. Nicholas as the patron or protector of their new homes. In Holland, SINTERKLAAS arrived by boat on the morning before St. Nicholas Day. Wearing a bishop's long robe, he rode a white horse through Amsterdam in a large parade. Dutch children left their wooden shoes near the hearth, along with straw and carrots for the horse.

Kris Kringle

In like manner, the Swiss immigrants brought the Christ Child tradition to America in the 18th century. Their version of the gift-giver was the young CHRIST CHILD who arrived on a gray or white mule with presents. Children left straw for the mule and nuts and cookies. Over time, the child was transformed into KRIS KRINGLE.

Père Noel

French settlers went to Midnight Mass on Christmas Eve, followed by a huge dinner called Reveillon. They enjoyed meat pies, poultry or duck, suet pudding, stews, and cakes. Children left their shoes by the fireplace, and PÈRE NOEL, the French Father Christmas, would leave sweets, small toys, fruits, and nuts.

Belsnickle

During the 19th century, German people contributed to the idea of the Santa Claus we know today. The fierce-eyed BELSNICKLE takes his name from Pelz Nicholas, meaning "St. Nicholas in fur." Often he wore a big fur coat, carried a black sack, and could be scary-looking. He carried goodies and treats for good children, and switches for children who had not been so good.

In other parts of Germany, however, an angelic messenger called CHRISTKINDL, known as a representative of the baby Jesus, left gifts for children. Early Christmas trees often had a picture or a doll figure tucked in the branches. Likely this idea is how we got the custom of an angel on top of the tree.

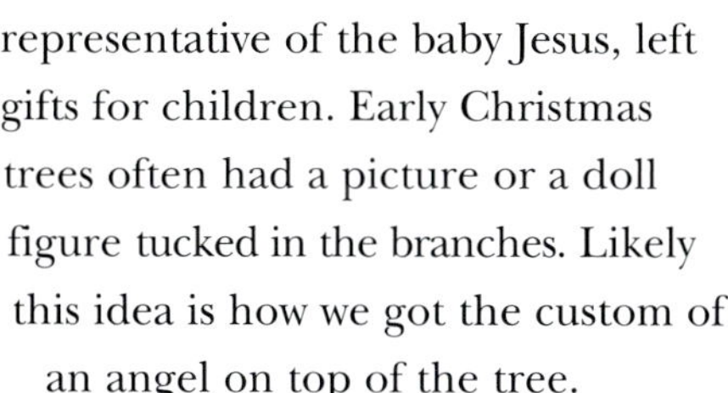

Christkindl

Children in Italy believe in LABEFANA, the female Santa dressed as a peasant woman. On the eve of January 5, a figure on a broomstick flies across the sky. She goes down chimneys and fills children's stockings with treats. Legend says that three kings journeyed through Italy in search of the Christ Child. They asked directions from a woman sweeping her cottage and invited her to join them. She turned them down, but later changed her mind. She packed a basket with food and gifts for the child and tried to follow the Magi or kings. She never found them, but still searches, looking carefully at every sleeping child to see if he is the Christ Child. As she travels, she leaves a gift, realizing that Christ can be found in all children.

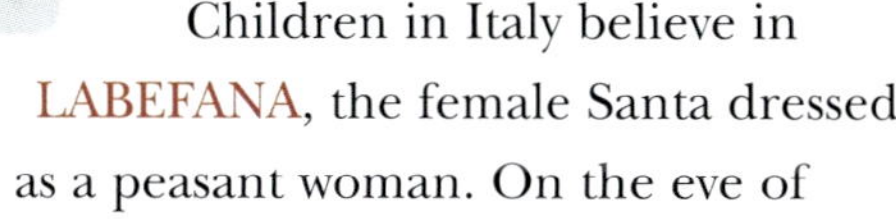

LaBefana

For Scottish people, Christmas Day meant attending church. There was no partying until Hogmanay or New Year's Eve. Just after midnight, men went "first footing," another way of giving gifts. The Scots believed that the first person entering a home in the new year would bring good or bad luck to the home for the coming year. If he had dark hair, that meant good luck; if he had red hair it meant bad luck.

On Christmas Eve in Sweden, a Christmas gnome or TOMTE emerges from his home under the floor of the house or the barns. He carries a sack over his shoulder and leaves gifts for all. Decorations include candles, apples, Swedish flags, small gnomes with tasseled caps, and straw ornaments. Swedish children today wait for Jultomten, a gnome whose sleigh is drawn by the Julbok, the Christmas goat. The tomte dresses in red and carries a bulging sack on his back.

Tomte

The Santa Claus we know today evolved from the works of three men—a scholar, a political cartoonist, and a commercial artist. In 1822, Clement C. Moore wrote a poem, *The Night Before Christmas,* which depicted a plump, bearded Dutchman traveling through the snow on the streets of New York City.

Political cartoonist Thomas Nast created a drawing of Santa talking on the phone to a little girl in 1884. It was based on his childhood memories of "A Visit from St. Nicholas."

In 1931, the Coca-Cola Company wanted to link its product with the merry feelings associated with Christmas. Commercial artist Haddon Sundblom created the familiar Santa figure, and a different ad was produced each year from 1931 to 1966.

Personal Expressions & Sweet Sensations

Whether you love to cook, craft, or decorate, let Santa play a part in your creativity as you celebrate the season.

A sleigh made of gingerbread holds holiday cookies for the wonderful season.

Holiday Bracelets

FIND A FAVORITE HOLIDAY SCRAPBOOK PAPER, SOME SIMPLE JEWELRY FINDINGS, AND ADD SOME HAPPY CHRISTMAS MESSAGES TO MAKE SWEET BRACELETS TO GIVE FROM SANTA.

What You'll Need

- Two coordinating scrapbook papers
- Metallic paint pen in silver, black, and/or gold
- Laminating film (self adhesive or office supply lamination)
- Pinking shears
- Hole punch
- ⅛-inch eyelets
- Eyelet setter and hammer
- Charm
- Jump rings
- Clasp set
- Long nose pliers (two pairs are best)
- Double-sided tape
- Scissors
- Ruler
- Pencil

Here's How

1. Measure out and cut five rectangles of scrapbook paper 1×½-inches. Accent the edges of the rectangles with the metallic silver paint pen if desired.
2. Print words on a coordinating scrapbook paper using a word processor, or hand write with a fine black or gold marker. Cut the words out so they fit within the rectangles. Attach the back of the rectangles to the coordinating paper using double-sided tape.
3. Laminate each rectangle. Trim with pinking shears if desired. Punch a hole in the laminating material on both short sides of each rectangle. Attach an eyelet using the setter and hammer. Cut the excess laminate around the rectangle leaving a small trim (margin) of laminate around it.
4. Connect the rectangles with jump rings using long nose pliers. Attach clasp set and charm with jump rings.

Paper Cone Santa Ornaments

BEND SOME PAPER AND CURL SOME RIBBONS AND YOU MIGHT FIND THAT YOU HAVE CREATED YOUR VERY OWN PAIR OF SANTAS.

What You'll Need

- Four coordinating scrapbook papers
- Cream-colored scrapbook paper
- White corrugated scrapbook paper
- Double-sided tape
- Transparent tape
- Fine black marker
- Hole punch
- Wire 20 gauge or higher
- Scissors

continued on page 148

Here's How

1. Make two copies of the patterns provided or trace the pattern twice using a pencil and tracing paper.
2. Lay one Santa pattern on main scrapbook paper and cut out. Lay one Santa leg pattern on scrapbook paper and cut out. Cut the Santa head pattern out of cream scrapbook paper. Using a duplicate copy of the Santa and Santa leg patterns, cut all of the small parts (boots, mittens, hat, etc.) out of scrapbook paper. (You can also cut out the arm, cuff and mitten in one piece of paper and then attach the cuffs and mittens in different paper over the top using double-sided tape.) Use hole punch to make paper buttons.
3. Attach the Santa beard, hat, etc. to the cream color Santa head using double-sided tape. Use a fine black marker to draw the eyes and nose. Attach the cuffs and mittens to the arms using tape also.
4. Attach the boot cuffs and boots to the Santa legs using double-sided tape. Attach the paper trim to Santa's coat.
5. Bend and coil Santa's coat into a cone shape and hold in place with double-sided tape. Attach Santa's head, arms, and buttons to the coat. Punch a hole in the top of the Santa legs. Thread wire through the hole and twist one end to secure. Thread wire up through the top of the cone and form a small loop for hanging the ornament. Twist wire in place and cut off excess (Tip: If wire slips the top of cone too easily, thread a small bead or button on the wire to stop the slippage.)
6. Hang the ornament with ribbon as desired or display sitting on books or other flat surface.

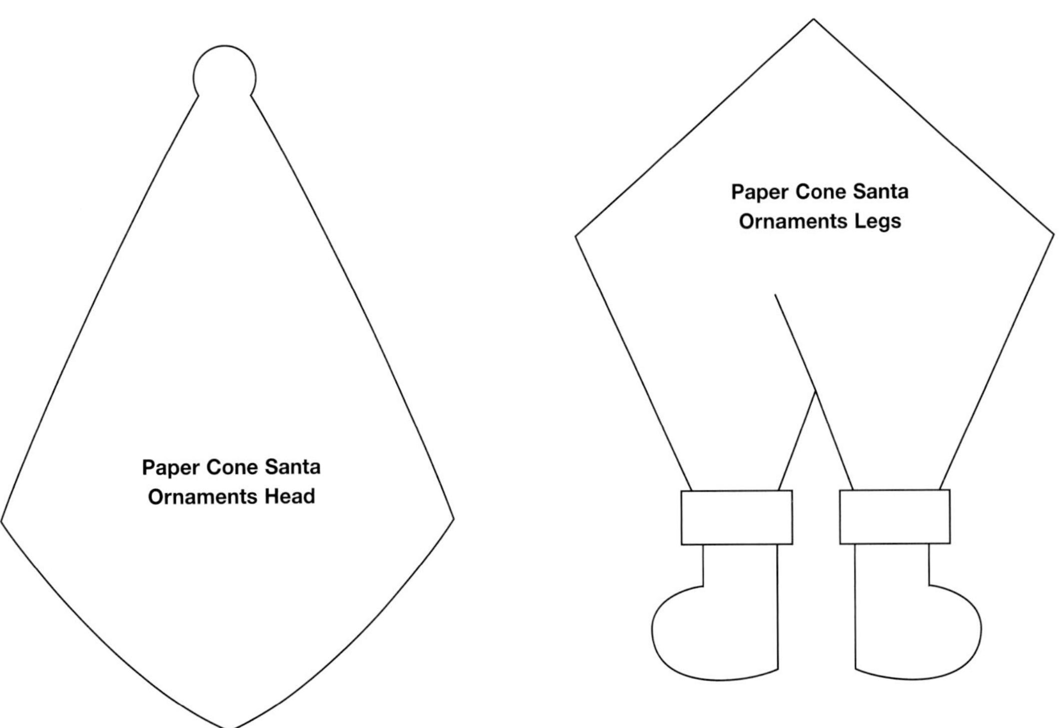

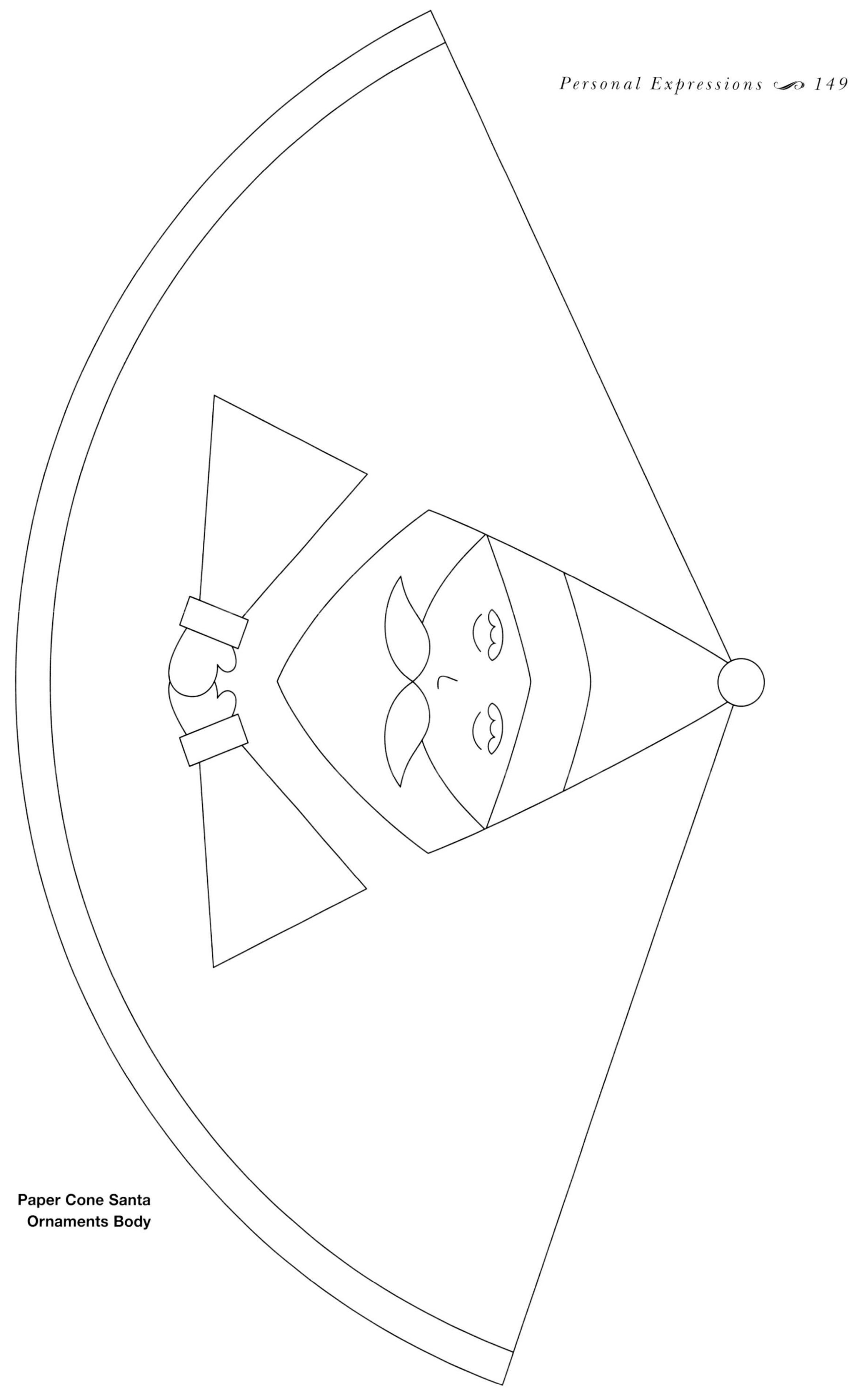

Paper Cone Santa Ornaments Body

Roly-Poly Santas

These cute fellows are round and plump—just the way Santa should be! Hint: Press the balls of dough against each other as you flatten them, so they won't separate after baking.

- **1 cup butter, softened**
- **½ cup sugar**
- **1 tablespoon milk**
- **1 teaspoon vanilla**
- **2¼ cups all-purpose flour**
- **Red paste food coloring**
- **Miniature semisweet chocolate pieces**
- **Red cinnamon candies**
- **Snow Frosting**

1. Preheat oven to 325°F. In a large bowl beat butter with an electric mixer on medium to high speed for 30 seconds. Add sugar; beat until combined, scraping sides of bowl occasionally. Beat in milk and vanilla. Beat in as much of the flour as you can. Stir in remaining flour. Remove 1 cup of dough. Stir red paste food coloring into remaining dough to make desired color.

2. Shape each Santa by making one ¾-inch ball and five ¼-inch balls from plain dough. From red dough shape one 1-inch ball and five ½-inch balls. Flatten the 1-inch red ball on an ungreased cookie sheet until ½ inch thick. Attach the plain ¾-inch ball for head and flatten until ½ inch thick. Attach four ½-inch red balls for arms and legs. Shape remaining ½-inch red ball into a hat. Place plain ¼-inch balls at ends of arms and legs for hands and feet and at top of hat. Add chocolate pieces for eyes and buttons.

3. Bake in preheated oven for 12 to 15 minutes or until edges are lightly browned. Cool on cookie sheet for 2 minutes. Transfer to wire racks; cool completely.

4. Spoon Snow Frosting into a decorating bag fitted with a medium star tip. Pipe mustache, beard, cuffs, and hatband. For nose, attach a cinnamon candy with a small dab of frosting. Allow frosting to dry. Makes 12.

Snow Frosting: In a small bowl beat ½ cup shortening and ½ teaspoon vanilla with an electric mixer for 30 seconds. Gradually add 1⅓ cups sifted powdered sugar, mixing well. Add 1 tablespoon milk. Gradually beat in 1 cup sifted powdered sugar and enough milk (3 to 4 teaspoons) to make a frosting of piping consistency. Color frosting as desired with paste food coloring. Use a decorating bag and star tip to pipe frosting in areas where texture is desired.

To Store: Place in layers separated by waxed paper in an airtight container; cover. Store at room temperature for up to 3 days or freeze undecorated cookies for up to 3 months. Thaw, then decorate cookies.

Candy Cane Cookies

Chocolate candy canes are delightful!

- **⅓ cup shortening**
- **⅓ cup butter, softened**
- **¾ cup sugar**
- **1 teaspoon baking powder**
- **1 egg**
- **2 tablespoons milk**
- **1 teaspoon vanilla**
- **⅓ cup unsweetened cocoa powder**
- **1¾ cups all-purpose flour**
- **4 ounces semisweet chocolate**
- **2 to 4 teaspoons shortening**
- **½ to ⅔ cup crushed peppermint candy canes**

1. Beat the ⅓ cup shortening and the butter on medium speed for 30 seconds. Beat in sugar and baking powder. Beat in egg, milk, and vanilla. Beat in cocoa powder and as much flour as you can. Stir in remaining flour. Divide dough in half. Cover dough and chill at least 1 hour.
2. Preheat oven to 375°F. On a lightly floured surface roll one portion of dough at a time to slightly less than a ¼-inch thickness . Use a 4-inch candy-cane-shape cutter to cut dough. Place cutouts 1 inch apart on an ungreased cookie sheet. Bake in preheated oven for 7 to 9 minutes or until firm and light brown. Transfer cookies to a wire rack; cool.
3. For drizzle, heat chocolate and 2 teaspoons shortening over low heat until melted, stirring often. (Add more shortening, if necessary, to make a drizzle of desired consistency.) Drizzle a few cookies with baking bar mixture; sprinkle with crushed candy canes. Repeat with remaining cookies. Let cookies stand until set. Makes about 36.

To Store: See instructions for Roly Poly Santas, page 150.

Elves' Hats

These cookies have had many names such as Peanut Butter Blossoms or Black-Eyed Susans, but at Christmastime they look just like elves' hats.

- ½ cup shortening
- ½ cup peanut butter
- ½ cup granulated sugar
- ½ cup packed brown sugar
- 1 teaspoon baking powder
- ⅛ teaspoon baking soda
- 1 egg
- 2 tablespoons milk
- 1 teaspoon vanilla
- 1¾ cups all-purpose flour
- ¼ cup green coarse sugar
- Milk chocolate kisses or stars

1. Preheat oven to 350°F. In a large bowl beat shortening and peanut butter with an electric mixer on medium speed for 30 seconds. Add the ½ cup granulated sugar, brown sugar, baking powder, and baking soda. Beat until combined, scraping sides of bowl occasionally. Beat in egg, milk, and vanilla. Beat in as much of the flour as you can with the mixer. Stir in any remaining flour.
2. Shape dough into 1-inch balls. Roll balls in the coarse green sugar. Place balls 2 inches apart on an ungreased cookie sheet.
3. Bake in preheated oven for 10 to 12 minutes or until edges are firm and bottoms are lightly browned. Immediately press a chocolate kiss or star into center of each cookie. Transfer to wire racks; cool.

Makes 54 cookies.

To Store: See instructions for Roly Poly Santas, page 150.

Kris Kringles

Pick your favorite color of cherry center for these special holiday cookies.

- ½ cup butter, softened
- ¼ cup sugar
- 1 egg yolk
- 1 teaspoon finely shredded lemon peel (set aside)
- 1 teaspoon lemon juice
- 1 cup all-purpose flour
- 1 tablespoon finely shredded orange peel
- 1 slightly beaten egg white
- ⅔ cup finely chopped walnuts
- 13 whole candied red or green cherries, halved

1. In a medium bowl beat butter with an electric mixer on medium to high speed for 30 seconds. Add the sugar; beat until combined. Beat in egg yolk and lemon juice. Stir in flour, orange peel, a dash of salt, and lemon peel. Cover and chill for 1 hour or until dough is easy to handle.

2. Preheat oven to 325°F. Shape dough into 1-inch balls. Dip balls in egg white and then roll in nuts. Place on a greased cookie sheet. Press a cherry half into each ball. Bake in preheated oven for 20 minutes or until lightly browned. Transfer cookies to wire racks; cool. Makes about 26 cookies.

To Store: See instructions for Roly Poly Santas, page 150.

Yule Logs

Symbolic of a Yule log on a blazing fire, these sweet and spicy little cookies add to the warmth and fellowship of the season. Note: If you like, use your favorite chocolate frosting instead of the Brown Butter Frosting.

- **1 cup butter, softened**
- **¾ cup granulated sugar**
- **¼ cup packed brown sugar**
- **½ teaspoon ground nutmeg**
- **½ teaspoon ground ginger**
- **1 egg**
- **1 tablespoon dark rum**
- **1 teaspoon vanilla**
- **3 cups all-purpose flour**
- **Browned-Butter Frosting**
- **Ground nutmeg**
- **Colored decorators sugars**

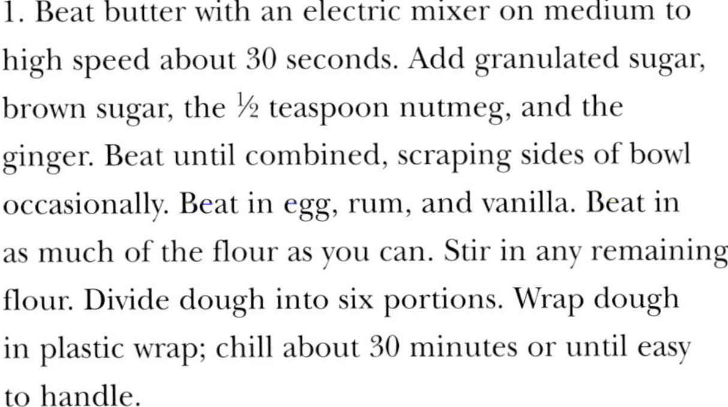

1. Beat butter with an electric mixer on medium to high speed about 30 seconds. Add granulated sugar, brown sugar, the ½ teaspoon nutmeg, and the ginger. Beat until combined, scraping sides of bowl occasionally. Beat in egg, rum, and vanilla. Beat in as much of the flour as you can. Stir in any remaining flour. Divide dough into six portions. Wrap dough in plastic wrap; chill about 30 minutes or until easy to handle.

2. Preheat oven to 350°F. On a lightly floured surface, shape each dough portion into a rope ½ inch thick. Cut ropes into 3-inch-long logs. Place logs 2 inches apart on an ungreased cookie sheet. Bake in preheated oven about 12 minutes or until lightly browned. Transfer cookies to wire racks; cool.

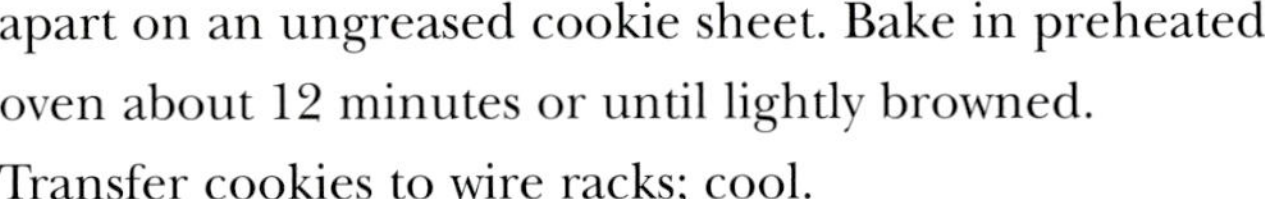

3. Spread Browned-Butter Frosting over each cookie. Run a fork lengthwise along log so frosting resembles bark. Sprinkle lightly with nutmeg and colored sugars. Let frosting dry. Makes about 48.

Browned-Butter Frosting: In a small saucepan heat ½ cup butter over low heat until melted. Continue heating until butter turns a delicate brown. Remove from heat; pour butter into a bowl. Beat in 5 cups sifted powdered sugar, ¼ cup milk, and 2 teaspoons vanilla until combined. Beat in enough milk (1 to 2 tablespoons) to make frosting of a spreading consistency.

To Store: See instructions for Roly Poly Santas, page 150.

Santa's Hats & Mittens

Cozy and cute, make them in all kinds of colors.

- **1 recipe Sugar Cookie Cutouts dough (recipe, page 153)**
- **Mitten-, and hat-shape cookie cutters (See Sources, page 158)**
- **1 recipe Royal Frosting (recipe, page 153)**
- **Paste food coloring in desired colors**
- **Coarse sugar**
- **⅛-inch-wide ribbons in assorted colors**
- **Colorful winter scarf**

1. Prepare Sugar Cookie Cutouts as directed, cutting out a total of 12 mitten and hat shapes. Before baking, use a drinking straw to make a hole near the top of each cutout. (Cut out remaining dough in desired shapes, bake, and reserve for another use.)

2. To decorate, place ½ cup Royal Frosting in a small bowl. Stir in additional warm water (2 to 3 teaspoons) to make frosting of glazing consistency. Spread glaze over cookies. Let completely dry about 2 to 3 hours.

3. In separate bowls, tint ¼-cup batches Royal Frosting

with desired food colorings. Transfer tinted icings to separate decorating bags fitted with tiny star tips. Pipe desired patterns onto cookies. While icing is still wet, sprinkle with coarse sugar. Let icing dry completely (about 4 hours). Makes about 3 dozen cookies.

To Store: See instructions for Roly Poly Santas, page 150.

Sugar Cookie Cutouts

Cut them in any shape you wish—they all taste good!

- ⅓ cup butter, softened
- ⅓ cup shortening
- ¾ cup sugar
- 1 teaspoon baking powder
- 1 egg
- 1 teaspoon vanilla
- 2 cups all-purpose flour

1. In a medium bowl, beat butter and shortening on medium to high speed for 30 seconds. Add sugar, baking powder, and a dash of salt. Beat until combined, scraping sides of bowl occasionally. Beat in egg and vanilla until combined. Beat in as much of the flour as you can with the mixer. Stir in any remaining flour. Cover; chill for 1 hour or until dough is easy to handle.
2. Preheat oven to 375°F. On a lightly floured surface roll a portion of the dough ⅛ inch thick. Cut out dough with well-floured cutters in desired shapes. If you plan to hang or assemble the cookies for decorative display, use a drinking straw to make holes in cutouts as needed.
3. Place cutouts 2 inches apart on ungreased cookie sheet. Bake in preheated oven for 8 to 10 minutes or until edges are firm and bottoms are very lightly browned. Cool on cookie sheet 1 minute. Using a straw, remake any holes that have baked shut. Transfer cookies to a wire rack and let cool. Repeat with remaining dough. Makes about 3 dozen 2½-inch cookies or about sixteen 5-inch cookies.

Note: If you feel the cookies will soften in the weather outdoors, hang the displays indoors or use them as tabletop decorations.

Royal Frosting: Combine 1 16-ounce package powdered sugar, sifted (4½ cups), 3 tablespoons meringue powder (find with cake decorating supplies at crafts stores), and ½ teaspoon cream of tartar. Add ½ cup warm water and 1 teaspoon vanilla. Beat with an electric mixer on low speed until combined; beat on high speed for 7 to 10 minutes or until mixture is very stiff. Cover with a damp paper towel and plastic wrap; refrigerate up to 2 days. Makes about 5 cups.

Visions of Sugar Plums

Use red paste food coloring rather than pink for a different look.

- 1 recipe Sugar Cookie Cutouts (recipe, page 153)
- Pink paste food coloring
- ¼ cup pastel non-pareils

1. Prepare Sugar Cookie Cutouts as directed. Divide dough in half. Tint one dough portion with red food coloring. Knead almonds into other portion. Cover and chill dough portions for 1 hour or until firm. Divide each portion in half.

2. On lightly floured tea towel, roll a red dough portion into a 12×8-inch rectangle. On waxed paper, roll an almond dough portion into a 12×8-inch rectangle. Invert almond rectangle over red rectangle; peel off paper. Roll up, starting from a long end. Pinch to seal. Wrap in plastic wrap. Repeat with remaining portions. Chill 1 to 2 hours or until firm.

3. Preheat oven to 375°F. Lightly grease cookie sheet. Remove one roll from refrigerator. Unwrap; reshape, if necessary. Cut into ¼-inch-thick slices. Place about 2 inches apart on prepared cookie sheet. Bake in preheated oven for 8 to 10 minutes or until tops are set. Transfer to a wire rack and let cool. Repeat with remaining dough roll. Makes about 65.

To Store: See instructions for Roly-Poly Santas, page 150.

Gingerbread Cutouts

Dark and rich and yummy—make lots!

- ½ cup shortening
- ½ cup sugar
- 1 teaspoon baking powder
- 1 teaspoon ground ginger
- ½ teaspoon baking soda
- ½ teaspoon ground cinnamon
- ½ teaspoon ground cloves
- ½ cup molasses
- 1 egg
- 1 tablespoon vinegar
- 2½ cups all-purpose flour

1. In a large mixing bowl, beat shortening on medium to high speed for 30 seconds. Add sugar, baking powder, ginger, baking soda, cinnamon, and cloves. Beat until combined, scraping sides of bowl frequently. Beat in molasses, egg, and vinegar. Beat in as much of the flour as you can with the mixer. Using a wooden spoon, stir in any remaining flour. Divide dough in half. Cover; chill about 3 hours or until easy to handle.

2. Preheat oven to 375°F. Grease cookie sheets; set aside. On a lightly floured surface, roll half of the dough ⅛ inch thick. Cut out dough with well-floured cutters in desired shapes. If you plan to hang or assemble the cookies for decorative display, use a drinking straw to make holes in cutouts as needed. Place cutouts 1 inch apart on prepared cookie sheets. Bake for 5 to 6 minutes or until edges are light brown. Cool on cookie sheets for 1 minute. Transfer to wire racks; cool. Repeat with remaining dough. Makes about thirty-four 5-inch cookies.

Note: If you feel the cookies will soften in the weather outdoors, hang the displays indoors or use them as tabletop decorations.

Gingerbread Reindeer

Make enough to pull Santa's sleigh!

- 1 recipe Gingerbread Cutouts dough (recipe, page 154)
- 1 5¾×5 ¼-inch deer-shape cookie cutter
- 1 recipe Royal Frosting (recipe, page 155)
- Red paste food coloring
- Silver and pastel dragees

1. Prepare Gingerbread cutouts as directed, cutting out eight deer shapes. (Cut out remaining dough in desired shapes, bake, and reserve for another use.)

2. To decorate, place ¼ cup white Royal Frosting in a decorating bag fitted with a writing tip. In separate bowl, tint ¼ cup Royal Frosting with green food coloring. Transfer to separate decorating bag fitted with writing tips. Using white and red icings, pipe outlines and details on the

deer. Pipe additional details around necks with white icing. Decorate with dragees. Let icing dry completely (about 4 hours). Makes about 34 cookies.

To Store: See instructions for Roly-Poly Santas, page 150.

Gingerbread Sleigh

Build this beautiful sleigh in no time with easy pattern pieces.

- ½ cup shortening
- 2½ cups all-purpose flour
- ½ cup sugar
- ½ cup molasses
- 1 egg
- 1 tablespoon vinegar
- 1 teaspoon baking powder
- 1 teaspoon ground ginger
- ½ teaspoon baking soda
- ½ teaspoon ground cinnamon
- 1 teaspoon ground cloves
- 1 ounce clear red hard candy, finely crushed
- Royal Frosting
- Materials:
- 2 8¾-inch-long red-and-white-striped candy canes (¾-inch diameter)
- 6 3½-inch-long red-and-white-striped candy sticks
- 4 green-striped square hard candies and 4 red-striped square hard candies (from a bag of mixed hard candies)
- 2 small red gumdrops
- 2 large red gumdrops
- Silver dragees (for decorating only; do not eat)
- 1 4½-inch-long red-and-green-striped candy stick or one 5¾-inch-long red-and-green-striped candy cane

1. Beat shortening in a mixing bowl with electric mixer on medium to high speed for 30 seconds or until softened. Add about half the flour, the sugar, molasses, egg, vinegar, baking powder, ginger, baking soda, cinnamon, and cloves. Beat until thoroughly combined. Beat in remaining flour. Cover and chill 3 hours or till easy to handle.

2. Cutting and baking: Enlarge the pattern pieces on heavy paper as directed on page 157.

3. For back of sleigh: Line a baking sheet with foil. Using a floured rolling pin, roll one-fourth of dough ⅛ to ¼ inch thick on the foil-lined baking sheet. Lay pattern for back of sleigh on dough. Using a sharp knife, cut around pattern and cut out design. Carefully remove excess dough; reserve for re-rolling.

Carefully spoon crushed candy into holes. Bake in a 375° oven for 5 minutes. Remove from oven and add additional candy. Bake 5 to 7 minutes more or until edges are lightly browned. Lay pattern on hot cookie and trim side and bottom edges, if necessary. Let cool completely on baking sheet. Remove foil.

4. For the other pieces: Roll half of the remaining dough to ⅛- to ¼-inch thickness on an ungreased baking sheet. Lay remaining pattern pieces on dough, leaving at least ¼ inch of space between pieces. Cut around pattern pieces and remove excess dough.

Bake in a 375° oven for 8 to 10 minutes or until edges are lightly browned. Lay pattern pieces on hot cookies and trim edges, if necessary. Let cookies cool 2 minutes; loosen with spatula but do not remove from pan. Cool completely.

5. Decorating pieces: Fit a decorating bag with a #3 writing tip; fill with Royal Frosting (recipe, see below right). Working on a waxed-paper-covered work surface, outline the red candy windows on the back of the sleigh. Let dry.

Add a few drops of red food coloring to ½ cup Royal Frosting; spoon into decorating bag fitted with #4 writing tip. Outline kick board; pipe swirl design in center. Outline both sidepieces of sleigh.

Fit #6 writing tip on white frosting bag. Pipe a line inside red line on top edges only. With red frosting, pipe series of dots ¼ inch apart inside white line. Pipe a loop from front edge to center of line of dots and on to back edge of each piece. Place silver dragees on soft frosting with edges touching. Let dry 2 hours.

6. Assembling the sleigh: Place the base of the sleigh on a waxed-paper-covered work surface. Position the sides, back, and kick board, holding them in place with inverted glass measuring cups and inverted custard cups or canned goods. (Note that the sides, back, and kick board angle out from the base.) When pieces are correctly positioned, use Royal Frosting in a decorating bag fitted with a #16 or #17 star tip to cement the pieces in place. When frosting is partially dry, add additional rows of frosting inside the sleigh to reinforce the seams. Cement the seat in place with frosting. Let the sleigh dry at least 2 hours.

7. While the sleigh is drying, assemble the runners. With a sawing motion, cut the curved end of each 8¾-inch-long cane at center of curve. (Candy canes and sticks cut more easily while still wrapped.) Place a large red gumdrop on the cut end of each. Set canes aside.

Cut four of the 3½-inch-long candy sticks in half. Position four of the pieces in a shallow W-shape against each remaining 3½-inch stick with cut ends against the stick. Cement with dollops of frosting. Cement two green square hard candies where the short pieces join each 3½-inch stick.

Place dollops of frosting on the short pieces at the opposite ends from the 3½-inch sticks. Place 8¾-inch canes atop, using extra sticks to support the ends of the canes. Let dry at least 2 hours.

8. Place the sleigh on its side. Attach a runner to the bottom of the sleigh with a generous line of frosting. Cement two green square hard candies where the short pieces join the 3½-inch stick. Let dry at least 2 hours.

Turn the sleigh to the other side and repeat with the other runner and remaining hard candies.

9. Using a decorating bag fitted with a #16 or #17 star tip and forming shell shapes, pipe a line of Royal Frosting from the center of the back of the sleigh to each front edge.

Pipe a line of frosting on the top edge of the kick board. Place a 4½-inch-long candy stick on frosting. Cement a small red gumdrop at each end of candy stick.

Store the completed sleigh in a dry place so frosting doesn't soften.

Royal Frosting: Combine 2 egg whites, 3 cups sifted powdered sugar, ½ teaspoon vanilla, and ¼ teaspoon cream of tartar in a small mixing bowl. Beat with electric mixer on high speed for 7 to 10 minutes or until the mixture is very stiff.

Keep the bowl covered with wet paper towels at all times to prevent the frosting from drying as you work. The frosting can be refrigerated overnight in a tightly covered container. Stir before using. Makes 2 cups.

Gingerbread Sleigh Patterns

1 square = 1 inch

Sources

BETTY LOU BYRNES *Pages 110-121*
Naperville, IL 60565
630/416-1463
dblbyrnes@wideopenwest.com

MARY ENGELBREIT *Pages 92-101*
www.Maryengelbreit.com

HOLLY JOY HOWE *Pages 64-71*
North Platte, NE 69101
308/534-6609
1000words@charter.net

JUDITH KLAWITTER *Pages 82-91*
Coeur d'Alene, ID
Judith@klawitter.com
www.jklawitter.com

JEAN LITTLEJOHN *Pages 132-139*
Clyde, NC 28721
828/627-0445
ncsantamaker@brinet.com

LEE MIDDLESWART *Pages 102-109*
Indianola, IA 50125
515/961-4094

WENDY MULLEN *Pages 38-47*
San Juan Bautista, CA 95045
831/623-1681
Wendy@victorianchocolatemolds.com

BRIAN PILKINGTON *Pages 14-21*
Reykjavik, Iceland
011-354-551-3297

EVELYN SCHIRM *Pages 54-61*
Urbandale, IA 50322
515/276-3323

PAT SEIFERT *Pages 48-53*
Urbandale, IA 50322
515/278-4794

JIM SHORE *Pages 122-131*
Heath Springs, NC 28743
c/o www.enesco.com

SUZI SMITH *Pages 140-143*
Candler, NC 28715
828/667-3690
dollwizz@charter.net

DALE AND TAMARA WOODARD *Pages 72-81*
Box 112334
Tacoma, WA 98411-2334
253/396-0127
www.anaveta.com

ICELANDIC CHRISTMAS *Pages 14-21*

- didyouknow.cd
- *Christmas Trolls* by Jan Brett (Putnam, 1993)
- *The Truth About Santa Claus* by James Cross Giblin (Thomas Y. Crowell, 1985)
- www. Simnet.is/gardarj/
- www. Randburg.com
- www. Jolahusid.com
- www. Icelandtouristboard.com
- www. Christmas.com
- www. Nordicstore.com

Better Homes and Gardens®

COLLECTION

Editor: Carol Field Dahlstrom
Designer: Angie Haupert Hoogensen
Copy Chief: Terri Fredrickson
Publishing Operations Manager: Karen Schirm
Senior Editor, Asset and Information Manager: Phillip Morgan
Edit and Design Production Coordinator: Mary Lee Gavin
Editorial Assistant: Cheryl Eckert
Book Production Managers: Pam Kvitne, Marjorie J. Schenkelberg, Rick von Holdt, Mark Weaver
Contributing Copy Editor: Amy Spence
Contributing Proofreaders: Tom Blackett, Jane Carlson, Beth Havey
Cover Photographer: Jay Wilde
Photographers: Mike Jensen, Mark Bryant, Bill Hopkins, Andy Lyons Cameraworks, Jay Wilde, Scott Little
Technical Illustrator: Chris Neubauer Graphics, Inc.

MEREDITH® BOOKS
Executive Director, Editorial: Gregory H. Kayko
Executive Director, Design: Matt Strelecki
Senior Editor/Group Manager: Jan Miller
Associate Marketing Director: Steve Swanson
Marketing Manager: Wendy Merical

Publisher and Editor in Chief: James D. Blume
Editorial Director: Linda Raglan Cunningham
Executive Director, New Business Development: Todd M. Davis
Executive Director, Sales: Ken Zagor
Director, Operations: George A. Susral
Director, Production: Douglas M. Johnston
Director, Marketing: Amy Nichols
Business Director: Jim Leonard

Vice President and General Manager: Douglas J. Guendel

BETTER HOMES AND GARDENS® MAGAZINE
Editor in Chief: Karol DeWulf Nickell

MEREDITH PUBLISHING GROUP
President: Jack Griffin
Executive Vice President: Bob Mate

MEREDITH CORPORATION
Chairman and Chief Executive Officer: William T. Kerr
President and Chief Operating Officer: Stephen M. Lacy

In Memoriam: E.T. Meredith III (1933-2003)

ISSN: 1524-9794
ISBN: 0-696-22595-6

All of us at Meredith® Books are dedicated to providing you with information and ideas to create beautiful and useful projects. We welcome your comments and suggestions. Write to us at: Meredith Books, Crafts Editorial Department, 1716 Locust Street—LN112, Des Moines, IA 50309-3023.

If you would like to purchase any of our crafts, cooking, gardening, home improvement, or home decorating and design books, check wherever quality books are sold. Or visit us at: bhgbooks.com

God Bless Us
Everyone!